The royal brothers have shared so much in life, not least their love of sport and passion for their charities. Here they enjoy a personal moment at the Invictus Games in 2014. (Max Mumby/Indigo/Getty Images)

WELCOME

The two sons of Prince Charles and Princess Diana had the same family background and upbringing. The only difference between them was that one of them knew that he would eventually become a British monarch while the other knew that he would have no such defined role. He would have to find a niche for himself that fitted with everyone's expectations of a second-born royal son while at the same time supporting the institution of which his brother would eventually be head.

For Prince William and Prince Harry, the pressures that would normally weigh down an heir to the throne and his brother were compounded by the very public separation and then divorce of their parents and the tragic death of their mother.

The elder brother subsequently made the choice to embrace the part he was born to play and serve his country as his grandmother had done. The other took the path that he felt had been forced upon him by a rigid institution and a popular press that was hungry for salacious gossip. For more than half their lives, the brothers were there for one another – friends, co-conspirators, supporters of their sibling through the bad times and celebrants of their successes and achievements in the good ones. Gradually, though, they have drifted apart and now face lives shaped in markedly different ways.

The dilemmas and issues encountered by the two princes are perhaps higher profile than most, but they are nonetheless the same as those faced for centuries by families in the British aristocracy. The eldest son has always been destined to inherit everything and spend his life as patriarch of the family estates and custodian of its traditions. The second son has usually entered the church or the Army but has been expected to stand by in case anything should happen to incapacitate his elder brother. What has been added to these time-honoured ways for the current royal princes is the seismic upheavals in the modern world where the importance of royal duty and the respect in which the monarchy is held have been eroded. The establishment is having to adapt and change, a process begun by the boys' father, Prince Charles, in the 1980s, but not yet completed.

Clearly, no one thing leads a person down the route in life they find themselves taking. For Princes William and Harry there have been many influences – some greater than others – that have made them the men they are today and those are what we explore in these pages. ●

Sheena Harvey Editor

ISBN: 978 1 80282 762 0
Editor: Sheena Harvey
Senior editor, specials: Roger Mortimer
Email: roger.mortimer@keypublishing.com
Cover Design: Steve Donovan
Design: SJmagic DESIGN SERVICES, India
Advertising Sales Manager: Brodie Baxter
Email: brodie.baxter@keypublishing.com
Tel: 01780 755131
Advertising Production: Debi McGowan
Email: debi.mcgowan@keypublishing.com

SUBSCRIPTION/MAIL ORDER
Key Publishing Ltd, PO Box 300, Stamford, Lincs, PE9 1NA
Tel: 01780 480404
Subscriptions email: subs@keypublishing.com
Mail Order email: orders@keypublishing.com
Website: www.keypublishing.com/shop

PUBLISHING
Group CEO: Adrian Cox
Publisher, Books and Bookazines:
Jonathan Jackson
Published by
Key Publishing Ltd, PO Box 100, Stamford, Lincs, PE9 1XQ
Tel: 01780 755131
Website: www.keypublishing.com

PRINTING
Precision Colour Printing Ltd, Haldane, Halesfield 1, Telford, Shropshire. TF7 4QQ

DISTRIBUTION
Seymour Distribution Ltd, 2 Poultry Avenue, London, EC1A 9PU
Enquiries Line: 02074 294000.

CONTENTS

Already set to serve the country: four-year-old William and two-year-old Harry play at soldiers outside Highgrove House in Gloucestershire in 1986. (Tim Graham/Getty Images)

The Prince and Princess of Wales have a very natural approach to being members of the royal family. (Slawek Kozakiewicz/dreamstime.com)

William and Harry walk behind The Queen's coffin on the day of her funeral in 2022. (Triumph0828/dreamstime.com)

An excited William and Harry with their mother Princess Diana, about to embark on a Maid of the Mist boat trip to Niagara Falls while on a tour in Canada in 1991. (Tim Graham/Getty Images)

Prince Harry oversees the launch of the Invictus Games in the Hague in 2020. (Max Mumby/Indigo/Getty Images)

Princes William and Harry discuss some of the finer points of athletics during the Invictus Games in London in 2014. (Max Mumby/Indigo/Getty Images)

TO THE MANNER BORN

Being born into an historic royal lineage means growing up in circumstances and surroundings that very few other people experience, with a lack of freedom to choose your way of life and your destiny.

Prince William Arthur Philip Louis was born on 21 June 1982, 11 months after the marriage of his parents, Prince Charles and Lady Diana Spencer. He was a baby of royal firsts – the first time a direct heir to the British throne had been born in a hospital and the first to have his father present at the birth. When he was nine months old he became the first royal baby to be taken on an overseas tour when he went on his parents' official trip to Australia and New Zealand. He has been the first in direct line to the throne to go to secondary school at Eton in Berkshire, rather than Gordonstoun in Moray, Scotland where his father and grandfather went. While serving with the Royal Air Force he became the first senior royal since the 15th century to live in Wales.

The year he was born was the year of the Falklands Conflict and just a few days before he arrived the British Army recaptured the islands' capital, Port Stanley. There had been a severe recession in the two years previous and unemployment was climbing to a high of 14%.

A Second Son

Prince Harry was born Henry Charles Albert David, two years after his brother on 15 September 1984. He was a welcome second son, although allegedly his father had been secretly hoping for a girl, perhaps thinking about the close relationship he had with his sister Anne and how they had complemented and supported each other through childhood and beyond.

With both boys, Charles and Diana broke with previous custom and practice and introduced their sons to the British people straight away. The infants were cradled by their parents on the steps of the Lindo Wing of St Mary's Hospital, Paddington in London where the press and well-wishers had been lined up to snap images that would be sent around the world. This, they hoped, would satisfy some of the public curiosity and allow them some private time.

They wanted their children to grow up in a normal atmosphere and not one where they felt they could not express themselves. They wanted them to feel loved, physically with cuddles and attention and mentally by being supported and encouraged in anything they wanted to do. This was despite the fact that generally in the 1980s children were not encouraged to question their elders but to do as they were told and not talk back. If they were naughty they would be

Queen Elizabeth shows a four-year-old Prince Charles how to work a movie camera in the garden of Balmoral Castle in 1952. (Lisa Sheridan/Getty Images)

A six-year-old Diana Spencer pushes her little brother Charles on a swing at Park House near Sandringham in 1967, the year their mother left their father. (Hulton Archive/Getty Images)

geared towards character building and then, as now, creating future leaders.

Even when he was home from boarding school, Charles was separated from his parents for long periods of time. Both his mother and father had extensive daily royal duties and long overseas trips, on which he was never taken.

As an officer in the Royal Navy, Prince Philip received a posting to Malta in October 1949, when Prince Charles was only 11 months old. The Queen spent as much time as she could with her husband during his two-year term on the island, meaning that Charles was left in the company of nannies for much of his infancy and early childhood. From then until he went to boarding school at the age of eight, he saw his parents only intermittently, due to The Queen's extensive official commitments.

Travel in those days was often undertaken in the royal yacht *Brittania* and so a trip to Africa or Australia took many months. The Queen's grand tour of Commonwealth countries in 1954, when Charles was six years old, took six months and saw her travel as far away as New Zealand while her son and daughter, Anne, grew up at home in the care of a governess.

Because of his naval career, Philip hardly knew his son for the first two years of his life and later only during the school holidays if the royal couple were in the country at the time.

The young prince was, however, given many experiences to educate him in a rounded way, even if a lot of these outings did not involve his parents. He was taken to plays and concerts, museums and exhibitions and he was taught to ride and sail, fish and shoot, and enjoy walks in the countryside.

When he was at home, Philip's naturally forceful personality often manifested itself in what could seem to be bullying of his children. He was keen to 'toughen up' Charles but his approach could often have the opposite effect of terrifying the small boy. Later in life Charles described his relationship with his father, relating how his criticism of the boy, for a deficiency in behaviour or attitude, easily drew tears. Neither of his parents were physically demonstrative, greeting their children with handshakes rather than hugs even after a long spell apart. His mother, Charles felt, was not indifferent to him but she was detached, consumed by her responsibilities as head of state. ⊃

smacked and that was no different for William and Harry. Their nannies were allowed to discipline them and were expected to teach them manners, as good behaviour amongst grown-ups was of paramount importance for a royal child. Inevitably, though, they were spoilt, not least by their doting parents, and that led William to being a rumbustious toddler and Harry a rebellious teen.

The Young Charles

Prince Charles was brought up in an atmosphere that was more akin to Victorian times in respect of outward shows of affection. As heir to the throne he was exposed to a full range of formal and decorous behaviour expected of him from a very early age. He had a sensitive nature that did not cope well with what, in his day, was the rough and tumble and rigid discipline of the boarding school he was assigned. This was Gordonstoun in the highlands of Scotland, where his father and grandfather had been educated. The school motto *Plus est en vous* – 'There is more in you' – sets the tone for an establishment that aims to give its pupils resilience to overcome disappointments and cope with any manner of physical and mental challenges. In Prince Charles' schooldays in the 1960s, this philosophy was practised within a rigorous framework of hard work and tough play with no encouragement of

pupils to express themselves emotionally or have individual opinions.

Until the 1970s Gordonstoun ran a spartan regime of early morning runs wearing only pants and gym shoes followed by cold showers and lessons before you even got to breakfast. During the academic day there were breaks for military exercises and periods of complete silence. All was

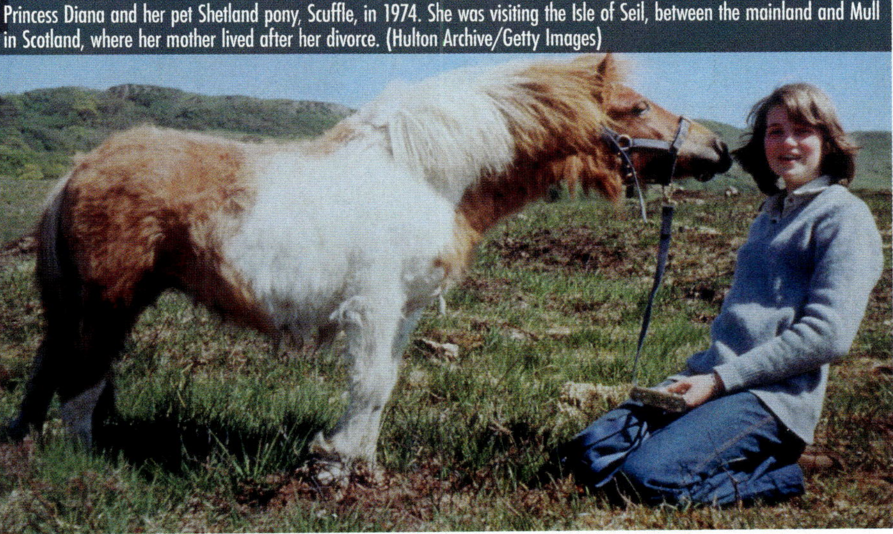

Princess Diana and her pet Shetland pony, Scuffle, in 1974. She was visiting the Isle of Seil, between the mainland and Mull in Scotland, where her mother lived after her divorce. (Hulton Archive/Getty Images)

Princess Diana's father, the 8th Earl Spencer, her stepmother Raine McCorquodale and young brother Charles on a visit to Buckingham Palace in 1981. (Gary Stone/Getty Images)

Diana's mother, Frances Shand Kydd and her sister Lady Jane Fellowes leave St Mary's Hospital in London in 1982, having met the newly born Prince William. (Mirrorpix/Getty Images)

It was this remote upbringing that led to Prince Charles' determination that his sons would know their father's affection and be guided by him through life rather than directed from afar.

The Young Diana

Although regarded as more of a 'commoner' than most royal spouses up to that point, Lady Diana Spencer was nonetheless a child of an aristocratic family. She was born and grew up in the 10-bedroomed Victorian manor Park House, on a country estate leased from the royal residence at Sandringham in Norfolk.

Diana was a contemporary of The Queen's two youngest children, Andrew and Edward, and they often played together when the royal family were in residence at Sandringham for the school holidays. The two houses were only about a mile apart, so it was easy for the boys to run over and join in swimming sessions in the pool or to watch a film.

Diana's father was the then Viscount Johnnie Althorp, later 8th Earl Spencer, and Frances Roche, daughter of Baron Fermoy – who was a close friend of King George VI. The Spencer family fortune dates back to Tudor times and sheep farming and trading livestock in Northamptonshire and Warwickshire. The family has been involved in government and entwined with royalty since the 17th century when they fought for the Crown in the English Civil War. John Spencer, the 1st Earl Spencer, was given his title in 1765 when he was serving as a Whig Member of Parliament for St Albans in Hertfordshire. Diana was a family name held by John Spencer's aunt and his sister.

The connection with royalty continued into the 20th century and Queen Elizabeth attended Johnnie and Frances' wedding in Westminster Abbey in 1954. Diana arrived in 1961 following the births of two sisters and a brother who died shortly after he was born. Her remaining brother, Charles Spencer, came four years later. Growing up in Norfolk with two older sisters was a rough-and-tumble time for Diana. The children had horses and ponies, dogs, cats and a whole host of small pets, hamsters, gerbils and rabbits. The royal parkland of Sandringham was an adventure playground where they could climb trees and skin knees and the young girls became quite tomboyish. In time, all the children were sent off to boarding school. Although not particularly academic, Diana was quite artistic and gifted in music and dance. She left school at 16 but, in the time-honoured fashion of society girls, she attended a Swiss finishing school for a short while when she was 18.

The household at Park House consisted of half a dozen servants, including a cook and a nanny/governess when the children were younger. Diana, despite having a background of being waited on and having parents with considerable wealth, undertook a series of ordinary paying jobs to support herself in London. She became a nanny, taught dance, did cleaning jobs and worked as a hostess at parties. She was also employed as a teaching assistant at a nursery ➲

Prince Charles at home in Kensington Palace enjoying being a hands-on dad to one-year-old Harry and three-year-old William. (Tim Graham/Getty Images)

A two-year-old Prince William takes his father's hand at
Aberdeen Airport on the trip back to London from their summer
break at Balmoral in 1984. (Tim Graham/Getty Images)

Prince William lends a steadying hand to his little brother as he takes a few tentative steps in their playroom at home in Kensington Palace in 1985. (Tim Graham/Getty Images)

school, which was where she was when her engagement to Prince Charles was announced.

Unfortunately, the Spencer marriage was not a long-lasting or happy one. Diana later said that she saw her father strike her mother and there were many family rows. The unhappiness at home unsettled the young Diana and left her with a life-long feeling of insecurity and mistrust. When Frances eventually left her husband for businessman Peter Shand Kydd in 1967 she tried to take the two younger children with her but the Earl stopped that and gained official custody through the courts.

Thereafter, the Earl tried to raise his children by himself, but he was not equipped to be a hands-on dad or understand what a young daughter needed for a fulfilling life. So although they had a good relationship, when her sisters were away at school and her brother was much younger, Diana was left to entertain herself in the remote Norfolk home, mostly with servants for company.

In 1976, when Diana was 15, Earl Spencer remarried, to Raine McCorquodale, daughter of flamboyant romantic novelist Barbara Cartland. The new Countess Spencer was 45 years old and had a forceful personality. She did not get on with her stepchildren, who resented her taking over the family home and running it even before she married their father. Their poor relations led to her being given the nickname Acid Raine and when the Earl died his son, Charles Spencer, evicted her from Althorp.

A Marriage of Convenience

Prince Charles was under pressure to find a wife who would fulfil the accepted qualifications for the spouse of a future king – to be gracious and dignified, passive and unimpeachable and, most importantly, capable of providing an heir to the throne. These attributes combined, to the best of Charles'

A pair of rocking horses get the young princes off to a galloping start in their riding careers. (Tim Graham/Getty Images)

Prince William with his Shetland pony at Highgrove House in Gloucestershire in 1986. By the age of four he was already learning to ride – a pastime he has enjoyed all his life. (Tim Graham/Getty Images)

advisors' knowledge, in Diana Spencer, the youngest daughter of Earl Spencer of Althorp in Buckinghamshire. At 18, she was 12 years younger than Charles, but she had a spotless reputation and a pleasingly modest personality, so she was considered a good match. Charles, who believed he had found the love of his life in the wholly unsuitable, because she was already married, Camilla Parker Bowles, didn't enter into the plan without reservations. He told a friend: "It is just a matter of taking an unusual plunge into some rather unknown circumstances that inevitably disturbs me, but I expect it will be the right thing in the end. It all seems ridiculous, because I do very much want to do the right thing for this country and for my family – but I am terrified sometimes of making a promise and then perhaps living to regret it."

Unfortunately, Diana didn't fit into his world and her husband's devotion to duty was something she could not fully understand. For Charles, his work on household and estate matters and his many charities was non-stop. Even on holiday there were papers to read, letters to sign and speeches to write. Ultimately, the rivalry in the marriage between his need to dutifully fulfil all the requirements of his office and her desire to have the undivided attention of a home-loving family man drove a wedge between them that left one baffled and frustrated and the other miserable and depressed.

They did, however, share an ambition for their sons to have a normal life growing up. Charles relished being an active dad, present at his sons' births and spending as much time playing and coaching them as he could. Diana wanted them to experience 'real' life and took them to enjoy some of the fun of normal boys but also to see people less fortunate than themselves and appreciate that the world was not comprised mainly of privileged people.

A World Full of People

More than gaining an appreciation of how wealth and privilege set them apart from others, William and Harry also had to learn that they would probably never have the luxury of true privacy, not in the way ordinary mortals might expect to have. It's hard to conceive of what a crowded universe the young princes inhabited. Aside from a large extended family they were surrounded by nannies, bodyguards, special police, cooks, butlers, housekeepers, chambermaids, footmen, kitchen staff, drivers, gardeners, grooms, stable lads and lasses, equerries, farm workers, their father's valets and private secretary, their mother's ladies-in-waiting, dresser and hairdresser – the royal homes and gardens were full of semi-strangers pretty much 24 hours a day.

Even when they were on overseas visits or on private holidays there would be a pared-down entourage travelling with them. So it must have been near-impossible for two boys to enjoy ⟳

Prince Diana leads five-year-old Prince Harry down to the beach for a swim in his water wings in 1989. (Julian Parker/Getty Images)

The young princes enjoy a skiing holiday in Lech, Austria in 1991, learning on the nursery slopes and already showing competence in the sport at the ages of seven and nine. (Tim Graham/Getty Images)

Already performing royal duties, Princes Harry and William wait in smart suits with neat hair at Buckingham Palace for the arrival of Queen Beatrix of the Netherlands in 1989. (AFP/Getty Images)

the simple, private and exclusive time with their two parents that their contemporaries enjoyed. Nevertheless, the love their parents had for the boys was always there and expressed as far as their respective characters allowed it. Diana was a hugger and being physically close to her sons was important to her. On their trip to Australia just after William was born, she gave him the affectionate nickname of Wombat. And after a young William said that he didn't want to become king and Harry cheekily responded, "If you don't want the job I'll have it" she called him GKH for Good King Harry. Harry revealed that his father, on the other hand, always called him 'darling boy'.

Although both Charles and Diana tried to be hands-on with their children, first their official appointments and then their marriage break-up kept them from being as close by and caring for the boys as they would have wanted. That left the boys to fall back on each other for support and companionship. Shared experiences and emotions drew them close together.

When their mother died that empathy grew as they coped with their grief in the face of the regimented behaviour that was expected of them as royalty. Harry, in particular, looked to his older brother to be an anchor in a world that had turned upside down. He has recorded how, as they walked behind their mother's coffin to Westminster Abbey, he kept sight of William out of the corner of his eye and drew immense strength from knowing he was there.

To Harry, William was Willy, a brother-in-arms, a confidant, an advisor and a supporter, even if he sometimes resented him in a way a younger sibling does. To William, Harry was Harold – even though his given name was Henry – his younger brother with whom he would joke, play sport, guide and protect whenever necessary.

Coming into the Modern World

In the days of austerity in the 1980s, when the senior royals' conspicuous personal wealth and considerable stipend from the public purse began to be questioned, Prince Charles started to formulate plans for modernising the monarchy. He recognised that many of the age-old royal customs, expenditure and estate management practices were outdated and alienating to a sizeable percentage of the British public. The mystique of monarchy had dwindled in people's eyes, as had a large proportion of respect for the establishment.

What better fun to be had than getting together with your cousins and burying your mother in sand? Princes William and Harry being normal children on holiday in 1990. (Tim Graham/Getty Images)

So it was no longer possible to hold the press at arms' length and expect that newspaper editors would suppress any less-than-desirable information that leaked out about royal business. Hence the decision to manage, as far as possible, official access to the children and negotiate some privacy at other times – a strategy that worked only occasionally.

Unfortunately, the very public break-up of Charles and Diana's marriage, the damaging publication of her autobiography and the embarrassing revelations about his long-lasting affair with Camilla Parker Bowles undid much of the work that had been done to protect William and Harry from the media spotlight. The whole family was thrown into a turmoil of mistrust and jealousy that could not fail to have an impact on the two boys at their young ages.

Then came the tragic death of Princess Diana, the confused aftermath and the public approval ratings of the monarchy plunging to an all-time low. The Palace machinery quickly stepped up a gear and took urgent steps to rehabilitate The Queen's image in the eyes of ordinary people. It was very obvious that we were no longer living in an age when respect trumped over disdain when anyone from the royal family made a faux pas. It was open season as far as the more salacious elements of the press were concerned and this freedom to criticise would affect the whole family for the near future and lead to some major changes in the way the system worked.

Through all of this, Princes William and Harry sought guidance and support from many different quarters. ●

Part of Princess Diana's plan to allow her boys to enjoy the life of an ordinary child was to take them to places such as Thorpe Park in Surrey in 1993 to enjoy a log flume ride. (Julian Parker/UK Press via Getty Images)

FAMILY
INFLUENCES

While Princes William and Harry could not always rely on their parents to be there during their childhood, they were surrounded by a family network of people who appreciated the pressures and responsibilities of being a young royal.

Some of William and Harry's close family members became trusted mentors, looking out for the boys and helping to guide them. Particularly, the Queen Mother was one of the relations the princes turned to, first when their parents' public duties kept them from home for extensive periods and then during the marriage break-up and following Princess Diana's death. She had decades of experience of royal life and a strong character. She had raised her two daughters to treat their duties and service to the nation with grave seriousness, a philosophy The Queen carried her entire life. The Queen Mother also had a background of very happy family life.

Elizabeth Bowes-Lyon was not born into any form of royalty, although her family were aristocratic, with a long history dating back to 13th century Scotland. She was one of ten children and her father had a notable reputation of being a considerate employer who treated tenants and employees on his estates and in his coalmines very well. Elizabeth had a great sense of fun and loved the arts, music and gardening. She had also been brought up with a strong Christian faith. She was a traditional debutante but natural and unspoiled, whose mother had taught her to cook, keep house and make her own clothes.

Elizabeth had not had the 'top job' in her sights when she married Prince Albert of York in 1923 and became the Duchess of York. In fact, she refused Albert's marriage proposal twice because she was not enamoured of the idea of becoming even a supporting member in the royal family cast. Her husband was the second son and they expected that his duties would include representing his father and brother at occasional official events, touring factories and meeting businesspeople and diplomats at home and abroad. She would open fetes and visit hospitals and bring up their daughters at their town house in Piccadilly, central London, and at Royal Lodge within Windsor Great Park in Surrey. These were modest houses by comparison to the royal palaces, Royal Lodge having been accommodation for some officers

Prince Harry, in a pageboy outfit, walks with his aunt Lady Sarah McCorquodale to church in 1989 for the wedding of his uncle Charles Spencer. (Tim Graham/Getty Images)

Princess Diana and the two princes with their cousin and grandmother Frances Shand-Kydd on holiday in 1990 on Necker in the British Virgin Islands. (Tim Graham/Getty Images)

Frances Shand-Kydd is followed by daughters Lady Sarah McCorquodale, Diana and Lady Jane Fellowes while Prince Harry digs in the sand. (Tim Graham/Getty Images)

grandmother. Six months before she died they were at Balmoral together for the family holidays and at the time, like all teenagers, he was feeling disregarded by his elders. He sat beside her one evening with a drink before dinner, as he recalled in his autobiography. "Our conversation started out as lively banter, then evolved, gradually settling into something deeper. A connection. Gan-Gan was really speaking to me that night, really listening... She was my Gan-Gan. She was born three years before the aeroplane was invented yet still played the bongo drums on her hundredth birthday... She'd seen so much, knew so much, there was so much to be learned from her..."

When he was at Eton school Prince William often used to cross Windsor Park for tea with his great grandmother and listen to her instruction on how to conduct himself when he eventually inherited the throne. They had an easy-going relationship and were not above pulling each other's legs, even when the Queen Mother was quite elderly. William later talked about seeing his 101-year-old great grandmother just before he started university. "She said, 'Any good parties, invite me down.' I said yes, but there was no way. I knew full well that if I invited her down she would dance me under the table."

Both he and Harry had enormous respect for their great grandmother and appreciated what she brought to their lives. William has said: "She loved a good laugh, even if the joke was about her. Anything that was meant to be formal and went wrong she enjoyed. She would have a good giggle. She had such a young sense of humour. Every single thing that went wrong or was funny for any reason she laughed herself stupid about – it kept us all sane."

Diana's Sisters

Lady Sarah McCorquodale and Lady Jane Fellowes are Princess Diana's older sisters. Of all the royal relations, the two women have been closest to Princes William and Harry following the death of their mother. They have been present at all their family events, including Harry's daughter Lilibet's christening in America in early March 2023, when senior royal family members had declined the invitation.

While Diana was alive, Sarah sometimes acted as her lady-in-waiting and they often took their children on holiday together where they could just be children and enjoy their cousins' company building sand castles at the beach, away from prying paparazzi camera lenses.

Aside from the bride and groom's parents and his brother and sister-in-law, Diana's sisters were the only other close family in the official photograph of Prince Archie's christening.

Cousins to Rely On

Princess Anne's son and daughter, Peter and Zara Phillips, were a source of companionship and a steadying influence on the princes growing up. Although Peter was five years older than William and seven years older than Harry, he was nonetheless a partner in crime in playing practical jokes on other members of the family when he and his sister Zara were children on holiday at Sandringham and Balmoral. "So there was quite a gang of us growing up in that age and it was a lot of fun," he has said. "We caused quite a bit of mayhem and chaos but, fortunately, I don't think we broke too much."

Peter also fulfilled a role as peacemaker in some of William and Harry's natural childhood

from the Royal Household until Prince Albert moved in his family in Queen Victoria's time.

The Duke of York's accession to the throne as George VI following his older brother's abdication threw his wife and young family unexpectedly into a life in the limelight and a sudden regime of major responsibilities. George VI, or Bertie as his family knew him, had not been trained for the throne. He lacked confidence and suffered from a debilitating stammer that hampered public speaking. The Duchess became his stalwart support, comforting and cushioning him as far as she could from the rigours of kingship. Just before the Coronation she confided in her children's nanny, Marion Crawford. "We must take what is coming to us,

and make the best of it," she said, a resignation to life that she would pass on to her daughter, grandchildren and great grandchildren.

All of her experiences put the Queen Mother in a unique position when it came to relating to her great grandsons. She knew well the restrictions of royal life, but she also knew what it was like to live without such restraints. She was a firm hand, but she was also fun. She had a strong sense of duty but a practical approach to fulfilling it and she knew both sides of the fence – the life of a king and the life of a second son.

The young princes knew her as Gan-Gan, enjoyed her company and sought her advice. Although he was only 17 when she died, Prince Harry felt a strong connection to his 101-year-old

Prince William chats to his great grandmother at her 99th birthday celebrations in 1999. (PA Images/Alamy Stock Photo)

Princess Eugenie takes a phone call during a fundraising event at Canary Wharf in London in 2011. She has been close to her cousins all their lives. (Feature Flash Photo Agency/Shutterstock)

squabbles. It would have been unusual for two young boys not to have arguments and fights and their older cousin was a useful arbiter if things got too heated. He and his sister would occasionally join William for a drink and a music gig at one of the pubs local to Sandringham, as their home, Gatcombe Park, was not many miles away. These sessions sometimes ended in a lock-in where the cousins and their friends would enjoy a relaxing chat into the late night.

When Princess Diana died Peter played a vital role in keeping the princes occupied during the media frenzy leading up to her funeral. The family stayed at Balmoral and Peter took William and Harry out to the fresh air of the moors every day, keeping them away from televisions, the hubbub in the castle and the sympathetic eyes of the staff. He took them shooting, fishing and riding their all-terrain motorbikes, trying to maintain normal boyhood activities to take their minds off their bereavement. Many years later he became a buffer between William and Harry when their relationship broke down and there is speculation that he might do so again to try to effect a reconciliation in time.

After Diana's death Zara brought some much-needed joy into William and Harry's lives even though she was only a year and three years older than them, respectively. Prince Charles decided to take the boys skiing five months after their mother's death and Zara went too and helped to distract attention from the princes. She threw snowballs and larked about with them, posing with them for the disliked but inevitable royal photoshoot on the slopes. Royal biographer, Victoria Arbiter, commented: "She was there to take the focus off them, take the pressure off. They used to hate those photocalls but with Zara everything is more fun because she's so gregarious, she's great to have around because of her positive energy and zest for life."

The cousins share a love of horses and competitive riding and Zara, now married to ex-rugby star Mike Tindall, was also a big supporter of Harry's major project, the Invictus Games, taking part in a wheelchair rugby match as part of its launch publicity. She is godmother to Prince George and her three children often play with William and Catherine's three.

Matchmaker, Matchmaker

Harry has always been particularly close to his cousin Princess Eugenie, daughter of his uncle Prince Andrew and Sarah Ferguson, even though she is six years younger. Eugenie and her older sister Princess Beatrice grew up playing with the royal princes and had the same group of friends

as William and Harry in their late teens and early 20s. They have a shared-experience bond because of their respective parental marriage breakdowns and the associated surge of embarrassing press coverage. The Duke and Duchess of York divorced in 1996, the same year as Princess Diana died, so all four children went through a huge amount of grief at that time. Of all the members of the royal circle of family and friends the two girls must surely share the greatest empathy with their cousins William and Harry.

The young people's social circle later included Harry's long-term girlfriend Chelsy Davy both during and after their relationship ended. Eugenie's husband, Jack Brooksbank was educated at Stowe School in Buckinghamshire with Chelsy and he was general manager of one of the favourite London nightclubs frequented by the royal celebrity set.

It was a while after the break-up of his romance with Chelsy and when the cousins were on a skiing holiday in 2012 that Eugenie introduced Harry to his next serious partner, Cressida Bonas, who he dated for two years.

The four cousins attended each other's weddings and after Prince Harry and his wife Meghan

Markle stepped down from being working royals they stayed close, particularly to Eugenie. She has always been supportive of the couple and has often visited them in their Montecito home in California. She was the only royal to feature in the Netflix documentary made about them, *Harry & Meghan*, where she appeared on a bike ride and paddling in the sea with Prince Archie. In early 2023 it was rumoured that Eugenie and her husband were considering a move to the Los Angeles area. The private residential communities company Jack Brooksbank works for in Portugal also has a branch in California.

At King Charles' coronation in 2023, Harry fell back on his cousins Beatrice and Eugenie to be his companions as he walked up the aisle at Westminster Abbey at the beginning and end of the service. The revelations he made in his autobiography, *Spare,* published just three months before, aroused much press and public speculation as to his role at the coronation and the welcome the royal family would give him. Sitting together in the same row as his close cousins will have afforded the prince the warmth of support and a distraction from feeling a focus of attention and gossip. ●

Zara Tindall on her horse Class Affair taking part in a cross-country event in Norfolk in 2020. (SHP Photography/Shutterstock)

THE WEIGHT OF MAJESTY

Most of us are conscious of what our ancestors have left to us and what we hope to pass on. But few of us can appreciate the burden that centuries of royal history and duty can have on the shaping of a person's life.

The British royal family, in common with only a very few other royal families around the world, has a record of public service stretching back hundreds of years. Not all royal history has been laudable or heroic but, good and bad, kings and queens have reigned over the isles and the people who live in the UK have built up an expectation of monarchy.

The relationship of royals to commoners is complex. On the one hand Britons see the royal family as the flag-bearers of the nation; figureheads and non-political representatives of its heritage and industry, guardians of tradition and shining examples of the best of British character. On the other hand, it often seems we want nothing more than to reveal their feet of clay, prove they're just like every other person in the country, if it weren't for the fact that they have wealth and privilege and somehow the right to rule.

The Queen managed to personify the country's expectations of the former, while much of the press has been in constant search for the latter, aided by a curious public lapping up every gossipy insider secret.

Into this hotbed of stiff upper lips and closely guarded private lives came the two princes, born to parents who ardently wanted them to grow up as normal human beings. But how could two people who can say they are the great-great-great-great-great-grandsons of Queen Victoria, and related through her to most of the crowned heads of Europe, who live in some of the largest and most venerated ancient houses in Britain, surrounded by world-famous artworks and furnishings worth millions, waited on by servants who bow or avert their eyes when they approach, hope to have a normal upbringing?

Brought up to know the grandeur of Buckingham Palace from the inside, play in its corridors and view the crowds from its famous balcony sets royal princes apart from all other children. (Walencienne/dreamstime.com)

For King and Country

Not only the general public but also each successive government of the country anticipates that a new generation of royals will continue the family tradition of service to the nation. Their public roles are expected to take precedence over any of their personal desires, commitments and ambitions. Their time is hardly ever their own; they are at the beck and call of politicians to impress foreign dignitaries and host diplomatic events, they are relied on to accept invitations to represent the business community and strengthen economic relations abroad, support the arts and be patrons to charities. They are invited to attend everything from gallery openings to rock concerts, but all in an official capacity, not for their sheer enjoyment.

The British Armed Forces have long had a close relationship with members of the royal family, as commanders-in-chief or as service personnel. These roles, at least, fitted with the interests of the two princes, both of whom successfully qualified as pilots and took part in active service. Harry, in particular, found freedom in being in the army for ten years and conducting two tours of duty in Afghanistan where he was treated as just one of the squaddies.

However, military service and in the case of William subsequent employment with the Norfolk Air Ambulance, have been the only real 'work' they have been able to do. Unlike many of the minor royals, they have not been expected to earn a living or have a career beyond supporting the monarch. They have been expected to be available at a moment's notice for royal duties and not tied down to a nine-to-five job.

Those duties, for major and minor royals alike, are many and varied. Around 3,000 UK organisations have a member of the royal family as their patron or president, giving the institution support and turning out to represent it whenever necessary. There are about 2,000 official engagements a year that require the presence of a royal. And 70,000 people every year are entertained at royal receptions, garden parties, lunches and dinners, while letters from 100,000 individuals receive a reply from the royal support team, with input from the family. It is a giant mechanism that rarely, if ever, pauses for breath, and being caught up in the midst of it is what Princes William and Harry have experienced since they were born.

Of course, being royals has given them the opportunity to initiate forces for good in areas to which they feel closest. For Prince William this has been in homelessness, environmental matters, wildlife protection and the future of the planet. For Prince Harry it has been in making a difference to children in southern Africa orphaned by the Aids pandemic, improving the standard and availability of sports training for young people, and supporting wounded servicemen through his Invictus Games, giving purpose, drive and dignity to those who have lost limbs and faculties in the defence of their country. Both princes have also been involved in mental health campaigns and raising awareness of mental health issues, something

As head of the royal family, The Queen set the standard expected of the princes — the tone of duty and service to the people, dignity and impartiality that dominated her reign. (Carnegie42/dreamstime.com)

their own life experiences have brought them close to appreciating.

The other side of the royal responsibilities coin is the fact that the family receives money from the Sovereign Grant in return for undertaking public duties, to help with the staffing and upkeep of ancient royal buildings, pay for transport costs and living expenses involved in performing their work. The Sovereign Grant is a percentage of the profits made by the Crown Estates. These are lands and holdings in the United Kingdom once owned by the monarch but now an independent commercial business belonging neither to the royal family nor the government. This arrangement dates back to 1760 and the reign of George III, who agreed ➲

King George VI, Queen Elizabeth, Princess Elizabeth and Princess Margaret Rose with ladies-in-waiting and uniformed footmen at the king's coronation in 1937, showing the formality and majesty that influenced the future Queen. (Getty Images)

to surrender his income from the Estate in return for an annual fixed payment. The rest of the profit from the Crown Estates goes to the British Treasury.

The royal family also has a private income from lands and businesses it owns but the Sovereign Grant imposes a particular onus on them to be seen to be earning this public money.

In the Limelight

In doing their work, both behind the scenes and in front of crowds, the two princes are also expected to be highly visible and allow themselves to be photographed so that everyone can see how well they are looking, what they are wearing, who they are with and to whom they are talking. A system has grown up whereby choreographed photoshoots are traded for some periods of anonymity, but this has only come about because of the damaging excesses of the past. And just because these arrangements are sometimes successfully negotiated doesn't mean that William and Harry have ever had the luxury of forgetting they are royals and what that means for how they live their lives.

Even when he was serving with the army as an Apache helicopter pilot in Afghanistan, Prince Harry could not live a completely normal life. As he said in an interview in the *Guardian* newspaper at the time: "For me it's not that normal because I go into the cookhouse and everyone has a good old gawp, and that's one thing that I dislike about being here [in the large military base Camp Bastion] because there's plenty of guys in there that have never met me, therefore look at me as Prince Harry and not as Captain Wales, which is frustrating."

Contributing to this has been the modern cult of celebrity. Television and social media have brought the royals so far into our homes that we feel we know them intimately and there's a temptation to treat them like members of our own family and a belief that they're fair game for criticism because they are 'our' royals and we pay for them. They are expected to make themselves available, do 'walkabouts' and always be upbeat and approachable. They're not supposed to have off days or bad moods. When you are always

The family traditions of pomp and ceremony into which the two princes were born are never more obvious than on the salute to the people from the balcony of Buckingham Palace on the occasion of Trooping the Colour in 2015. (Samir Hussein/WireImage)

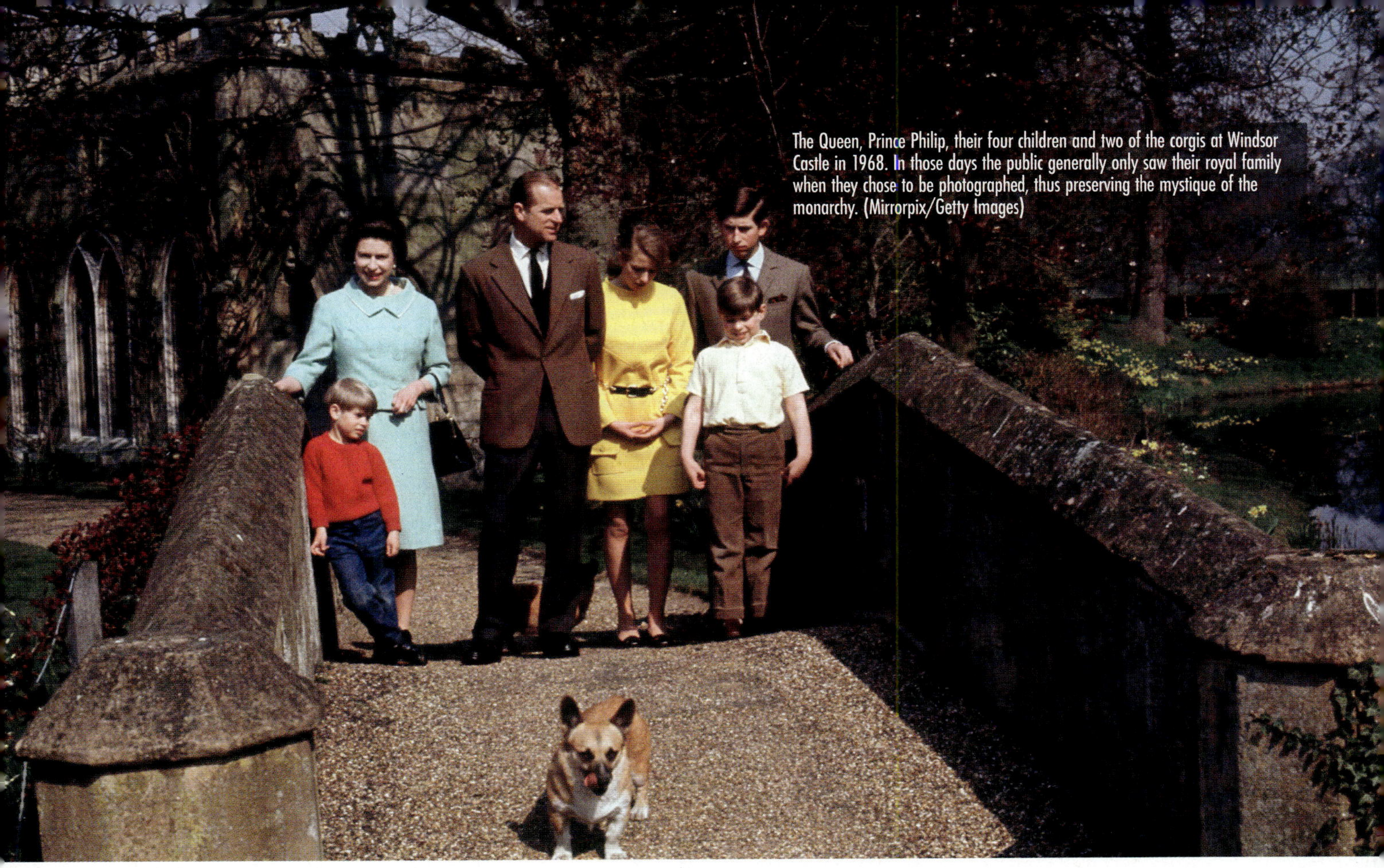

The Queen, Prince Philip, their four children and two of the corgis at Windsor Castle in 1968. In those days the public generally only saw their royal family when they chose to be photographed, thus preserving the mystique of the monarchy. (Mirrorpix/Getty Images)

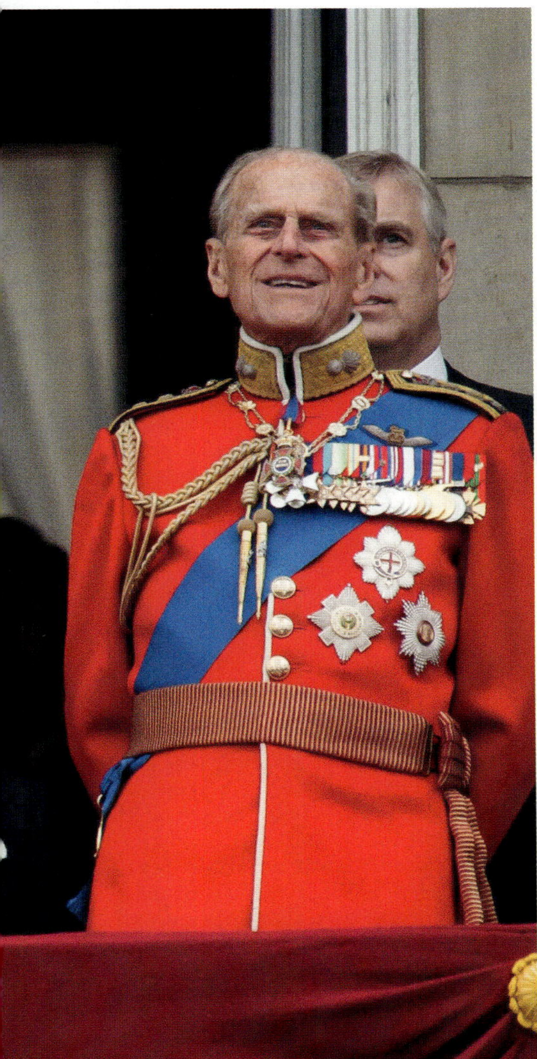

on display and don't have a right to reply to unpleasantries, this must impose pressure that's difficult to handle.

Perhaps if their parents had not had such a turbulent relationship, had their divorce not been so high profile and their mistakes and vulnerabilities not paraded so publicly, and had Diana not died so tragically, then the two princes might have been able to initiate a new, modern era of royalty, one less hidebound in tradition, as Prince Charles wanted. However, all of these events raised the stakes for a future king and his brother. The country wanted a royal family to be proud of, not one that was the subject of international gossip and contempt. So best behaviour was what was required and this added pressure drove a wedge through the family, dividing one who was willing to conform from one who had had enough of it all. ●

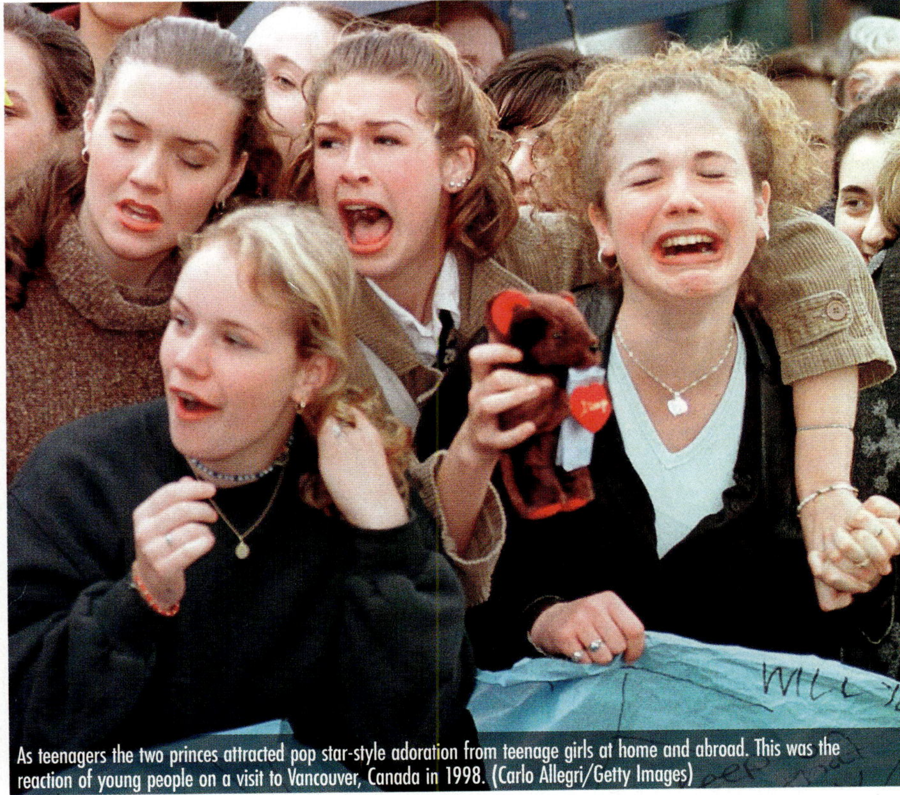

As teenagers the two princes attracted pop star-style adoration from teenage girls at home and abroad. This was the reaction of young people on a visit to Vancouver, Canada in 1998. (Carlo Allegri/Getty Images)

NANNY KNOWS BEST

Some of the strongest influences in a young royal's life are the women who stand in for both parents when their duties take them away from the home.

I n the homes of affluent businesspeople, landed gentry and aristocrats, it's customary for children to be brought up with nannies who take on a parental role when mother and father are occupied with work or public duties. In the case of well-known celebrities, high-profile politicians and royal families, a nanny is only one member of their children's household, which also routinely includes cooks, governesses, drivers and armed bodyguards who accompany their charges everywhere.

For Princes William and Harry, despite Princess Diana's desire to be as much of a hands-on mum as possible, several nannies played a big part in their upbringing. Their parent's official duties around the UK, their charity work and the calls on their time to attend evening receptions and make extended royal overseas visits meant that they could not be mother and father to the boys as consistently as happens in everyday families.

Princess Diana and Prince Charles always tried to be there for holidays, special occasions such as birthdays, school plays and sports days, but day-to-day neither of them could guarantee to be around to get the boys up and ready in the mornings, do the school runs, play with them, supervise mealtimes or tuck them up in bed at night. Those things mainly fell to the dedicated women who had charge of the princes from babyhood.

William's first nanny, who also looked after Harry for a short while after he was born, was Barbara Barnes, nicknamed Baba. She was the daughter of an estate worker at the Earl of Leicester's Holkham Hall in Norfolk, who had just come to the end of a 15-year tenure raising the children of the Hon Colin and Lady Anne Tennant, who was the daughter of the Earl and a friend to Princess Margaret.

Prince William's first nanny, Barbara Barnes, carries him off the plane at the end of his parents' tour of Australia and New Zealand in 1983. (David Levenson/Getty Images)

Although she had had no formal training as a nanny, Barbara came highly recommended by the Tennants who said she had a natural way with children and a genius for bringing out the best in them. At the age of 39, she was almost twice Princess Diana's age and experienced in handling young children with firmness but kindness. She had strong ideas on how children should be brought up, which included the wearing of sensible shoes and plenty of fresh air.

Her natural ways became clear in her determination not to wear the customary nanny uniform, her belief that each child must be treated as an individual, her encouragement of them to call her by her first name, and her sense of humour. She helped both princes learn to walk and talk, and played with them and comforted them if they hurt themselves or woke in the night. As a toddler, William adored her.

Unfortunately, the children's closeness to Baba caused strain between her and Princess Diana, which led ultimately to Barbara's departure from the royal household when William was four and a half years old. Harry was only two so he would not have been so aware of her leaving, but it must have had a devastating effect on William, suddenly losing someone who was so much a part of his young life and such an influence on his first formative years. It was an early taste of the loss he would endure ten years later when his mother died. Having been a quiet little boy he became boisterous, getting into playground fights, being cheeky and throwing the occasional tantrum.

New nannies

Barbara Barnes was replaced by two further, short-lived nannies. The first was Ruth Wallace, again not a qualified nanny but a trained nurse who had previously been a relief nanny to the children of Princess Michael of Kent. She was with the family for three years and it was she who coaxed Prince William out of his bullying behaviour at nursery school. He was a noticeably confident and strong-willed child whose sometimes questionable, self-centred conduct amongst his playmates had earned him the nickname 'Billy the Basher'. Like most first-born children on the arrival of a second child, he must have felt himself supplanted and acted badly as a result, even though he was popular and had lots of friends.

A change in the weather required nanny Wallace to issue a change of clothing to the two princes so they could watch their father play polo at Cirencester in 1987. (Tim Graham/Getty Images)

Harry, by contrast, was quite a quiet boy, who didn't make friends easily and needed encouragement to come out of himself. Ruth managed both diverse personalities so well they always held an affection for her and were reported to be shocked and saddened by her death in 2003 when she was only in her early 50s. While she was the children's nanny, Ruth was also a confidante of Princess Diana and although all the members of the whole family were fond of her, she found it difficult to cope with the atmosphere around the royal couple as their marriage began to break apart and so she left their employ.

Ruth was followed by Jessie Webb, who joined just at the point when William was going to his first boarding school and so she mainly took on the care of Harry, who was coming up six. She was a cheerful but no-nonsense person who believed in hearty eating for growing boys and treated William and Harry like normal children who needed strict guidelines and boundaries. She was not afraid to criticise any attempts to spoil or upset the princes and she was fierce in her protection of them. This was especially valuable for their mental health as her tenure coincided with much of the turmoil in the immediate lead-up to Prince Charles' and Princess Diana's divorce.

So fondly was Jessie remembered by William in particular, that he and Kate asked for her help with their new-born Prince George in 2013. She agreed, but only to cover the first few months until they found a suitable permanent nanny as by that time she was 71 years old.

After the divorce of the Prince and Princess of Wales, the two boys divided the time they were not in boarding school between their parents' homes. At that point Olga Powell stepped up to the position of Senior Nanny. She had

Dressed alike, Princes Harry and William watch the polo from the balcony at the Guards Club in Windsor with nanny Ruth Wallace in 1987. (Tim Graham/Getty Images)

William and Harry on the way to Sandringham Stables for a riding lesson with nanny Ruth Wallace in 1990. (Julian Parker/UK Press via Getty Images)

been a deputy nanny since William was six months old so she knew the boys very well. She was stern but fair, not above giving them a clip round the ear if they were naughty, but always loving and compassionate. She was the nanny William wrote to from boarding school to share his feelings when he was told that his parents were going to divorce, and she provided the loving arms to comfort the two bereaved boys in the terrible days after Princess Diana's death. She was ferociously loyal to the royal family and never indulged in any conversations with anyone about what went on in the homes of her young charges.

Right up to her death at the age of 82 in 2012 she was a notable presence in both boys' lives.

She went to Harry's confirmation, William's 21st, his passing out parade from Sandhurst and his wedding. When she died, William cancelled a number of official engagements so that he could go to her funeral, representing not only himself and his wife but his brother, who was on a tour of duty in Afghanistan and could not return home. In her turn, she made plain her continued closeness to the princes by leaving instructions that mourners should donate what they would have spent on flowers to Harry's charity, Sentebale, which he founded to support children in Lesotho, Africa.

A Controversial Nanny

The last great influence in Prince William and Prince Harry's teenage years was Alexandra Legge-Bourke, known as Tiggy. Her mother was lady-in-waiting to Princess Anne and she had originally been hired as an assistant to Richard Aylard who was Prince Charles' Private Secretary from 1991 to 1996. Tiggy was in her late 20s and from 1993 became like a big sister to the princes. She was a perfect person to take charge of them when they had their turn at Highgrove House with their father. She picked them up from boarding school and, if Prince Charles was busy with official engagements, she would take them riding, walking and climbing, shooting and fishing, playing polo, go-carting,

Prince William casts a wistful backward look as his new nanny Jessie Webb leads him away from the action at the Guards Polo Club, Windsor, in 1990. (Tim Graham/Getty Images)

A sleigh ride for the two young princes in Lech, Austria, in 1993, accompanied by their mother and much-loved nanny Olga Powell. (Julian Parker/UK Press via Getty Images)

visiting friends and shopping. In the season they went skiing together and she once took them abseiling. With her tomboy ways, she was more like a jolly companion to the boys, particularly Prince Harry, rather than a traditional nanny. She helped them to have fun with healthy outdoor pursuits and amusements away from the glare of the media, at a time when their home lives were undergoing such public upheavals.

Unfortunately, being much closer than other nannies to Princess Diana in age, and getting along so well with the princes, Tiggy was resented by their mother. She was even accused of having an affair with Prince Charles and a false story circulated that she had fallen pregnant and had had an abortion. These lies were later found to have been a fabrication of the BBC reporter Martin Bashir who used them as leverage to gain the notorious tell-all *Panorama* TV interview with Diana in 1995.

Tiggy left royal employment on her marriage in 1999 and despite being disliked by their mother, has stayed very close to William and Harry. They both went to her wedding and stood as godfathers to her children. She is also rumoured to be one of Harry's son Archie's godparents, the names of whom have been kept a closely guarded secret. ●

A smartly dressed Prince Harry arrives at Aberdeen railway station en route to Balmoral with his father and nanny Tiggy Legge-Bourke in 1993. (Julian Parker/UK Press via Getty Images)

Tiggy Legge-Bourke, with the two princes and their father, steps down from the plane that has taken them to Klosters in Switzerland for a skiing holiday in 1994. (Julian Parker/UK Press via Getty Images)

Clutching his Thomas the Tank Engine lunch bag, four-year-old Prince William arrives home from nursery school with his bodyguard in 1986. (Tim Graham/Getty Images)

THE BODYGUARDS

The princes' other close companions, always at their sides and present throughout their lives, have been their Personal Protection Officers.

These people, mainly from military or police backgrounds, accompany all the senior members of the royal family around the clock as well as lower ranking royals when they travel on official business. Together with designated police officers at specific events, Personal Protection Officers (PPOs) ensure their principal's safety in the face of every threat, from an over-enthusiastic fan to a potential terrorist. In this respect, the royal family is no different to any other high-profile celebrities who attract undesirable attention throughout their lives and fear for their personal safety. The difference is the national importance of ensuring the monarchy's direct line of inheritance is not endangered, so SO14 Royalty Protection Group is an elaborate entity. It is an offshoot of the London Metropolitan Police Service Protection Command and is broken down into Personal and Close Protection, Residential Protection and the Special Escort Group.

PPOs are trained in unarmed combat, the use of firearms, anti-terrorism evasive driving, threat recognition and avoidance, and emergency first aid. They are always dressed discreetly and carry a 9mm Glock 17 pistol or Taser stun gun, two-way radio and first aid kit, as well as occasionally a stab vest. Prior to any event at which senior royals are attending, they undertake reconnaissance of the area and plan the management of the situation, contingency options and emergency evacuation processes. They are expected to put their lives at risk to protect their royal charges, if necessary. In return, they are well paid, with many of the royals' PPOs earning six-figure salaries.

Prior to 2017, PPOs were separated into two groups – one of which looked after the royal family and the other high-ranking politicians and diplomats. Those assigned to royal duties were in place for extended periods, long enough to get to

Prince William is accompanied by his bodyguard, Reg Spinney, as he leaves the piste on the family's Austrian skiing holiday in 1991. (Tim Graham/Getty Images)

know the people they were looking after and form friendly relationships with them. After 2017, the two groups were merged so that today protection comes from a pool of more than 150 operatives with less prolonged contact with the principals they are guarding, although in practice the senior royals still have their own designated officers.

The two other branches of the Met Police Service, Residential Protection and the Special Escort Group, are less about personal contact. Uniformed officers from the former patrol the royal residences, particularly when the senior royals are at home. Motorcycle officers from the latter take over when the royals are on the move, along with marked and unmarked police cars, organising motorcades, controlling traffic and clearing the way for the royal vehicles. They tend to be more heavily armed, sometimes carrying a single-fire Heckler & Koch MP5 sub-machine gun.

Spies and Spying

Apart from concealed weapons and covert radio communications, the life of a PPO is filled with other practices that have echoes of fictional espionage – senior royals, for instance, are given code names so that they can be entered in a PPO's phone without the risk of their numbers falling into unauthorised hands. The names are regularly changed, but at one time Prince William's alias was Danny Collins and Prince Harry was David Stevens, reflecting the initials of Duke of Cambridge and Duke of Sussex. ➲

Even something as innocuous as a summer school tea party required the services of minder Christopher Tarr – and formal dress! – in 1996 when Prince William was at Eton School. (Tim Graham/Getty Images)

Prince Harry's PPO goes above and beyond his contracted duties as he helps Prince Harry remove his boots after a charity polo match in 2006. Prince Charles' polo manager, Robert ffrench Blake looks on. (Max Mumby/Indigo/Getty Images)

Nevertheless, the royal bodyguards over the years have been companions as well, sharing in the boys' activities and helping them navigate through the world. Dressed in plain clothes and always just a few paces behind their charges, they have participated in school runs and ski trips, walks down Eton High Street and overseas charity trips.

From when they were small children their protection officers have been there for all their normal activities, participating in the school run to and from nursery and then in dropping and collection from boarding schools at term times. They were playmates to the children in their younger days and accompanied them to their sporting events when they were older, helping with their equipment and cheering their endeavours. They have often stood in 'loco parentis'. For example, when Prince William was at Ludgrove, one of his schoolmates accidentally hit him with a golf club and gashed his head. The school matron was all for taking him to the school sanitorium for treatment, but his PPO insisted that an ambulance be called. He was not leaving anything to chance in his responsibility for the prince. In the event, William had sustained a skull fracture that necessitated an operation to relieve pressure on his brain, so the determination of his protection officer may well have saved his life.

From dramas such as this, to more light-hearted moments, PPOs have been people whom the princes could trust, around whom they could be frank and act naturally, knowing that they were not passing judgement, were always supportive.

The aim of a personal protection officer is to be low-key, to not stand out but simply shadow their principal, ready to intervene in a situation if necessary. In this respect they are highly successful. Unlike Hollywood movies with FBI agents in sharp suits talking to their shirt cuffs, royal PPOs can often come across as a friend or older relation providing accompaniment rather than obvious protection. There are many stories of people bumping into royals such as Prince William, when he was using the local swimming baths and shopping in supermarkets at the time he was working as a rescue pilot for the RAF in Anglesey, and his bodyguards being mistaken for Air Force mates.

Former royal bodyguard, Simon Morgan, has said: "Bodyguarding is a thought process. Planning is the most essential aspect of the role... countless meetings about planning, journeys, telephone calls and more meetings to discuss how the journeys will work. It's not about fighting, driving, shooting, or looking good in sunglasses." Those 'hard skills' may come into play a small percentage of the time, but he said: "90% of the time you will be talking to people, understanding what is going on with a crowd."

According to Morgan, one of the biggest challenge for a PPO is a crowd. On walkabouts when royals go out to meet and greet the public or, as happened after the death of Princess Diana and The Queen, review the floral tributes and messages of condolence, there is great relief when they are safely back indoors or in the secure environment of a protected car. "There's an element of uncertainty despite the control. You're looking at everyone, wondering why someone is smiling or why someone is not smiling. You're looking for danger cues in individuals' behaviour and standard of dress, people's facial expressions... constantly observing and evaluating the information that's coming in to you."

Part of protection in circumstances such as these is having an understanding with the person being protected. A rule is that the protection officer will look out for and react to how the royal is feeling and another that the royal will respond as directed by the PPO at all times. There has to be non-verbal communication between the two so that the royal can discreetly indicate if they are uncomfortable or nervous and, on the reverse side, that the bodyguard can instantly remove them from the situation without argument if they sense danger.

PPOs have to be loyal and tight-lipped because they are privy to many private details and events in their principals' lives. A security officer's vow of silence is a mandatory aspect of the job. Knowing that they can be trusted, no matter what the circumstances, is important for vulnerable royals.

Never Alone

The result of the constant presence of PPOs is that William and Harry have rarely known a private moment alone. Psychologically, there must be an effect on your outlook on life to the thought that somewhere 'out there' is an ever-present danger that requires you to be protected.

A bodyguard each for the princes – Ian McRae (left) and Peter Brown – as they attend the opening of a fountain built in the memory of Princess Diana in 2004. (Tim Graham/Getty Images)

Personal Protection Officer Mark Dyer talks to Prince William, on his right, during a visit in 1999 to see the launch of 16 Air Assault Brigade at Wattisham Airfield in Suffolk. (Tim Graham/Getty Images)

Of course, they can't always fit the bill. When William was at St Andrew's university, the PPOs were given a room nearby his in the halls of residence. David Corner, who was the Registrar of the university, responsible for the students' non-academic welfare, recalled the protection officers prowling round the campus, attempting to keep a low profile. "They dressed like 70s' middle-class students – in cords and jackets," he said. "They stood out a mile trying to blend in and look like students." No guns were allowed on campus but they obviously got round it in some way as local people referred to an unmarked car that was often seen patrolling round the town as 'the gun van'.

At times, the two boys did put their PPOs in awkward situations, relying on their loyalty. When Harry was a teenager, for instance, he would like to join schoolfriends at the local pub, shadowed but never judged by his bodyguard. And although senior members of the royal family can never spontaneously nip out for a walk or go on a spur-of-the-moment shopping trip, William and Harry were able to achieve some impulsive moments with help from their not-always-delighted protectors.

On the eve of his marriage to Catherine Middleton, Prince William and his brother made an impromptu outing from Clarence House to talk and pose for photographs with the many people who had been camped out so they could catch a glimpse of the royal couple the following day. Royal Protection Officer, David Lombardi, later revealed that he facilitated the walkabout by doing what he called "a dynamic risk assessment" to decide that it would be safe and he then accompanied the princes to ensure everything would be all right. Having these men and woman on hand, a familiar face to rely on not just for safety but for companionship at isolated and lonely moments, must have been reassuring for princes who didn't always have the benefit of family around them. Small wonder, then, that Harry felt adrift when he left royal circles and could no longer call on such round-the-clock personal protection.

A Special Influence

One PPO was a steady presence in both princes' lives as they were growing up. Mark Dyer, nicknamed Marko, was present at some of the major moments – good and bad – of their teenage years.

Dyer is a former Welsh Guards officer, often referred to as Harry's 'second dad'. He began his association with the royal family as an equerry to Prince Charles in the mid-1990s. He provided a steady guiding hand to Harry in his rebellious teen years and was chosen by Charles to accompany his son on his gap year travelling abroad. He was there on trips to Argentina and Australia and the two months Harry spent in Lesotho in southern Africa. Harry describes him as: "the roughest, the toughest, the most dashing. Raconteur. Man's man through and through." His first experience of him was on a trip with William and their nanny/companion Tiggy Legge-Bourke to Botswana in his brother's Easter holiday break from Eton in 1999. In the hubbub of guides, trackers, drivers, cooks and porters that gathered at their bush camp, Harry remembers the solid presence of Marko: "...like a traffic cop, directing, cajoling, embracing, barking, laughing, always laughing."

The respect commanded by this larger-than-life man of his royal charges, gave him the standing to steady the princes when their antics were not compatible with their roles as heirs to the throne. He was one of the boys' bodyguards who was aware of illicit visits to pubs and cannabis smoking amongst their peer group, but he remained discreet and just kept a watchful eye on the princes' behaviour. Dyer organised a visit for Harry when he was 17 to a drug and alcohol rehabilitation centre in south London so that he could meet former heroin and cocaine addicts and hear their stories. The visit was nominally to teach the prince about the centre's work in the community but it must surely also have been Dyer's intention to expose his young protégé to a life-lesson in the consequences of taking drugs. ●

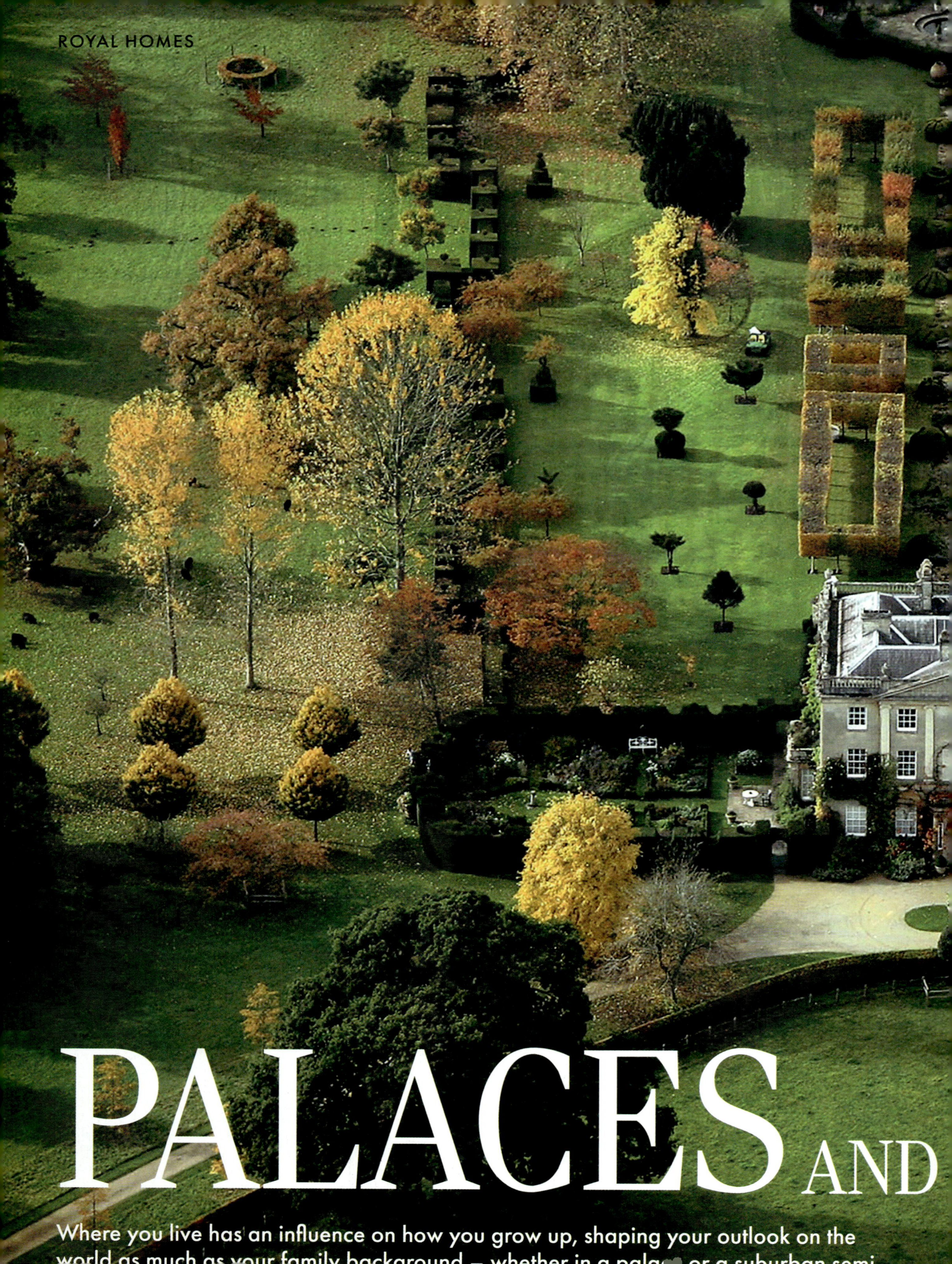

PALACES AND

Where you live has an influence on how you grow up, shaping your outlook on the
world as much as your family background – whether in a palace or a suburban semi.

The beautiful gardens of Highgrove House in Gloucestershire, seen in their autumn glory, were the holiday playground of
the young royals, and are Prince Charles' pride and joy. (Matt Cardy/Getty Images)

CASTLES

Being royal means inhabiting some of the country's grandest houses, surrounded by history and a fortune in precious artworks, antiques and designer furnishings. None of that will have meant much to two small boys, but living in a stately home and being aware of your parents' and grandparents' feelings of responsibility as custodians of the nation's heritage is a hidden pressure most children will never experience.

Although offering lots of space to grow and develop, vast, many bedroomed houses with ornate furniture must be difficult places to conjure an atmosphere of cosiness and security. Harry has said he was afraid to sleep with the door to his room closed when he was very young. In most of the homes the family occupied on rotation, depending on the time of year, the two princes were expected to stay in their nursery suite of rooms, where their nannies also had their accommodation. Unlike most other children, they did not often have the run of the houses as these places are largely multi-functional with office spaces and reception rooms for official entertaining where small boys are not welcomed.

Only at Balmoral Castle did they experience a freer childhood in fresh Scottish air with much less pomp and ceremony, rules and expected behaviours.

Kensington Palace

When they were married, Prince Charles and Princess Diana moved into newly refurbished apartments in Kensington Palace, the other side of Hyde Park from Buckingham Palace in central London. In 1689, King William III and Queen Mary bought the house – which was quite a modest size at the time – from the Earl of Nottingham as a place where they could be close to Parliament yet escape Whitehall Palace and the damp air from the River Thames

that was so bad for William's asthma. Famous architect Sir Christopher Wren masterminded the transformation of medium-sized house to palace by adding three-storey pavilions to each of the four corners of the original two-storey building, as well as new north and south wings. It contained separate King's and Queen's Apartments, in the southeast and northwest pavilions, as well as many other ornate state rooms, halls, galleries and grand staircases. It became an opulent place where the couple could hold parties, balls and dinners and entertain ambassadors and foreign royalty.

Queen Anne added a large orangery in 1705 for summer parties and the growing of exotic plants and trees. The names of the palace's creators reads like a *Who's Who* of architects and interior designers of the time, listing as it does not only Christopher Wren but Nicholas Hawksmoor, John Vanbrugh and Grinling Gibbons, who provided the internal pillars and carvings. George I added decorated ceilings, fine art and grand furniture. The very ornate King's Staircase, for instance, is flanked by painted walls depicting in life-size many of the important figures in King George's court.

Over the course of the next two monarchies – George II and George III – Kensington Palace declined. George III especially didn't like the building and so never lived there. He did, however, convert it into a series of private and grace-and-favour apartments for members of the Royal Household and to lend to some of his relatives, including his son Edward, Duke of Kent, who was the father of Queen Victoria. She was born there in 1819 and spent most of her childhood within its walls. When her uncle, King William IV died in 1837 she became Queen and held her first Privy Council meeting with her most senior ministers and advisors in the Palace's Red Saloon. A painting of that meeting still hangs in the Saloon, a constant reminder of the part the Palace has played in history. A statue of The Queen, designed by

her artistic daughter Princess Louise, sits in the formal gardens leading to the West Front.

Once Victoria had moved out to Buckingham Palace, Kensington Palace became almost a rest home for two of The Queen's daughters as well as other minor royals and retired loyal retainers, a trend that continued into the early 20th century. By that time the Palace was home to three of the Duke of Windsor's elderly royal relatives and so earned from him the nickname of the 'Aunt Heap'. The State Apartments were opened to the public while the inhabitants were housed in the numerous private apartments.

The Palace became more lively again when Princess Margaret, Lord Snowden and their children took up residence in the 1960s. Then the Prince and Princess of Wales, with Prince William and Prince Harry, made it their home in the 1980s, following in the footsteps of Prince and Princess Michael of Kent and their family, the Duke and Duchess of Gloucester and their three children and Diana's sister Jane and husband Robert Fellowes with their daughter, who all had accommodation there.

The nursery at Kensington Palace was almost a self-contained apartment with bedrooms, bathrooms, playrooms and a kitchen and dining room. The children spent most of their indoor time in these rooms, eating all their meals there with their full-time and part-time nannies, although they usually went down into the main part of the home to see their parents just before bedtime or if they were invited to meet visitors.

Highgrove House

King Charles' family residence was built between 1796 and 1798 near Tetbury in Gloucestershire. It was sold to the Duchy of Cornwall in 1980 by the son of former Prime Minister Harold Macmillan, who had been living there since the mid-1950s, and Prince Charles was given a tenancy-for-life by the Duchy. The location suited the future King because it is almost equidistant from London

The imposing gates of Kensington Palace shine in the sunlight. Bought by William III in 1689 as a small retreat in the country, it was gradually enlarged and surrounded by the urban expansion of London. (Peter Dazeley/Getty Images)

The formal gardens and fountains at the back of Kensington Palace with their summer flower display. (Irina Kershunova/Shutterstock)

and Cornwall. It is also only seven miles from Princess Anne's home, Gatcombe Park, and, perhaps more significantly in the 1990s, only half an hour's drive from Camilla Parker Bowles' marital home near Chippenham.

Highgrove has four main reception rooms, nine main bedrooms, six bathrooms and staff accommodation. As in Kensington Palace, there was a complete nursery suite of bedrooms and playrooms. Meals were made in the main house kitchen and delivered to the nursery wing on a tray. The difference between Highgrove and Kensington Palace was the extent of the grounds and the freedom the boys had to play in the gardens, parkland and surrounding woodland. Two public footpaths that originally ran through the estate were diverted when Prince Charles moved in so the boys could enjoy an amount of privacy for their games.

There was an outdoor heated swimming pool, a playground with swings and slide and in the cellar was a bomb-proof shelter, built for the future king's security, which the boys were allowed to use as a den and somewhere to have fun with their friends when they came to stay. They called it Club H and as they grew older it was decked out with a state-of-the-art music system.

Highgrove also encompasses an organic farm and the whole estate had become organic by 1994, far earlier than most thanks to Prince Charles' great interest in sustainable food production. The house and adjoining farm were also adapted to be as eco-friendly as possible, given it is a listed building, with a natural waste disposal system, heating via a wood chip boiler and solar panels on the farm roof.

The gardens at Highgrove are extensive and divided into a formal garden with topiary, statuary, willow sculptures and water features, a scented Carpet Garden, an arboretum,

Stumpery and cottage garden with classical-style wooden 'temples', a wildflower meadow and a walled kitchen garden.

All of these features combined to give the royal princes the best chance of informal living, learning about the countryside and farming and interacting with the working people on the estate. They spent much of their childhood weekends and school holidays, before and after their parents' separation and divorce and Princess Diana's death, at Highgrove. It was somewhere to host their friends and, occasionally, to go a little wild.

Balmoral

The relative privacy of a home in Gloucestershire was as nothing by comparison to the isolation of the imposing granite castle in the Cairngorms National Park in the highlands of Scotland, 50 miles west of Aberdeen and occupying 50,000 acres of working farm, forestry and grouse moors. There are seven hills over the height of 3,000ft (known as Munros) within the estate and a two-mile long freshwater loch.

The castle, with its decorative crenelations and fairy-tale towers, was built by Queen Victoria on land bought for her by Prince Albert, so it is private property and does not belong to the Crown, and the estate is managed by a board of Trustees. The building that now stands there replaced an older, smaller castle that was deemed by Prince Albert to not be big enough to house the extended royal family. The new castle ⮕

Princess Diana plays with the children on their slide and climbing frame in the gardens of Highgrove House in Gloucestershire in 1986. (Tim Graham/Getty Images)

The royal family pose in the wildflower meadow in front of Highgrove House in 1986. (Tim Graham/Getty Images)

Balmoral holidays were a chance for the princes to breathe fresh Scottish air and enjoy country life, but shortly after this picture was taken their mother was involved in her fatal accident and their whole world changed. (Tim Graham/Getty Images)

apparently has 52 bedrooms and very many reception rooms.

Also on the estate there is Birkhall House, which was built by Queen Victoria to house her staff but which is the preferred residence of King Charles, who inherited it from his grandmother, the Queen Mother, when she died in 2002. And there is Craigowan Lodge, a seven-bedroomed home a mile from the castle, which members of the royal family often choose as the more comfortable place to stay, as well as numerous farm cottages. Overall, there are more than 150 buildings on the vast estate.

Balmoral was Queen Elizabeth II's annual holiday home and it was there that Princes William and Harry were staying when their mother was killed in the Paris car crash. It is also where The Queen died in September 2022. While they were holidaying there, the royal family was free of public duties so the princes had more of their parents' and grandparents' attention and the chance to have fun with normal activities. There were family picnics – grilling venison steaks and sausages on a barbecue and doing the washing up – riding, fishing, shooting, reading books and walking dogs, without being surrounded by too many servants and security staff.

When their mother died, Queen Elizabeth decided the best place for the two boys to stay before and after the funeral was Balmoral, away from the glare of publicity and able to escape to the outdoors if they needed to be alone. There, Prince Charles was able to comfort them and they had the companionship of their nanny Tiggy Legge-Bourke and their uncle, Peter Phillips to distract their minds. But the wild Scottish countryside must have seemed very bleak to two bereaved young princes. ●

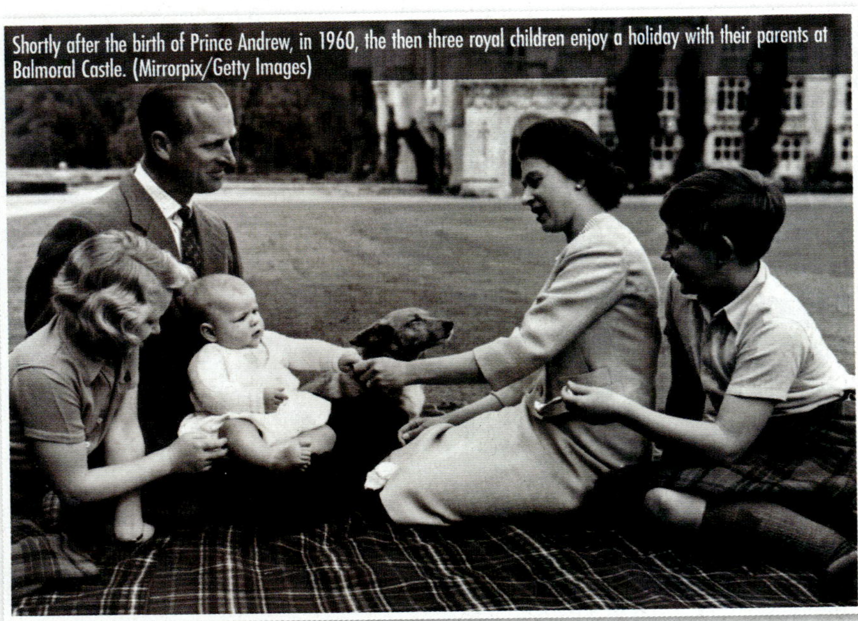

Shortly after the birth of Prince Andrew, in 1960, the then three royal children enjoy a holiday with their parents at Balmoral Castle. (Mirrorpix/Getty Images)

The walled rose garden at Balmoral Castle, the floral colours softening the building's austere granite exterior. (Universal Images Group/Getty Images)

SCHOOL DAYS

One of the greatest influences in a person's life is the education they receive, and going to school also helped the princes forge life-long friendships.

Princess Diana drops the boys off at Wetherby School in the Notting Hill district of London. It is Prince Harry's first day joining his big brother William at the school. (Tim Graham/Getty Images)

Cooking up a paella at Eton in 2000. Prince William had been brought up by his mother to be able to look after himself at home. (Ken Goff/Getty Images)

Until Prince Charles went to Hill House School in the district of Knightsbridge in west London at the age of eight, all royal children in the direct line to the throne had been educated at home by governesses and tutors and then at military academies. The choice of a civilian school was made by the royal couple on the advice of the then Prime Minister, Harold Macmillan. They felt that Charles needed the company of a classroom of children and the desire was that the prince be treated as a normal boy with no one showing him any deference as the son of the monarch. Shortly after he was sent to board at Cheam School in Hampshire and then Gordonstoun in the highlands of Scotland.

Although his school days were not wholly happy ones, due to his gentle temperament and sensitive nature, Prince Charles wanted the same normality for his two sons. This corresponded with Princess Diana's wish that the boys grow up in a conventional family atmosphere, not apart from their parents as both she and Charles had experienced. Diana had lost her mother at the age of seven when her parents separated. She had been educated at home in Park House near Sandringham, Norfolk, by a governess who formed a small group of local children into a class so that Diana would have some companionship her own age.

Diana's father was a man of his time, not equipped to replace a mother to a small child. Her two sisters were four and six years older and at boarding school, and her brother was just a toddler, so life at home must have been quite lonely. Then she went to boarding school herself and, like her sisters, only saw her father during the holidays when he was at home. Unlike Prince Charles, who was exposed to cultural experiences and outdoor activities, Diana was not taken to plays or on outings to the zoo, she rarely went to parties or dances and she knew ⮞

Prince William in the formal outfit of waistcoat and 'spongebag' trousers worn by Eton School's 21 elected prefects, charged with leading the younger boys by example. (Ken Goff/Getty Images)

Like students everywhere, Prince William spent many hours during his A-levels working at the computer in his room at the boarding house. (Ken Goff/Getty Images)

nothing of sports or country pursuits. This, despite spending all her time in either Norfolk or in Northamptonshire after her grandfather died and her father moved the family to the ancestral seat of Althorp House.

So, from both parents the push was for Princes William and Harry to feel loved and enjoy spending quality time with their parents. Nevertheless, it would have been exceptional in their circle of British society if the Prince and Princess of Wales had not sent their sons to boarding school.

The First Years

William and Harry's first experience of education was a year at Jane Mynor's Nursery School in west London (now the Minors Nursery School), on which they both embarked at the age of three. They were taught using the Montessori system favoured by Princess Diana, where there is an emphasis on children's freedom of choice and social development, learning through play and at their own pace. Teachers guide and encourage discovery rather than instructing their pupils, which set William, and later Harry, on the path of independent thought.

The next stage in their school career was Wetherby School in the Notting Hill

Prince Harry takes part in rehearsals for a tattoo at Eton in 2003. He was given the honour of Parade Commander, marching the 48-strong cadet Guard of Honour on and off the College Field with their colours. (Kirsty Wigglesworth-Pool/Getty Images)

Prince William in a pensive mood on his 18th birthday as he prepares to embark on a gap year prior to joining the University of St Andrews in Scotland. (Tim Graham/Getty Images)

district of London. This was a pre-preparatory establishment – the equivalent of an infant school – that in William and Harry's day took boys from four to eight years of age. It has since expanded to become a full prep school with students up to the age of 13. The school states its aim is: "...to ensure every boy has a happy and fulfilling experience". It believes boys should be well-rounded and confident learners who are respectful, thoughtful and kind, with integrity and good manners. A parent is quoted on the school website saying: "Wetherby boys are allowed to be boys; they are not punished for having a joke and fun or being rowdy during outside breaks, or being competitive at sport."

This philosophy must have chimed with both Prince Charles and Princess Diana, bearing in mind their own upbringings. The approach led to the boys learning how to behave with decorum befitting their station and position in life but also how to have fun and enjoy themselves with friends and playing physical games.

Wetherby was followed by Ludgrove Preparatory School where William arrived in 1992 at the age of eight, and Harry two years later. The school is a small, family-run boarding establishment in Berkshire. Ludgrove's motto is a quote from the Bible: "Whatsoever thy hand findeth to do, do it with all thy might". The headmaster and his wife at the time were Gerald and Janet Barber who made great efforts to imbue the school with a homely atmosphere where the pupils were encouraged to support each other. The school retains that ethos to this day, with emphasis placed on the children having a good rapport with their peers and with adults – a true preparatory experience to give them confidence, self-reliance and discipline when they graduate to secondary education.

The homely, supportive atmosphere was a blessing for the two boys because their parents had separated just before William started at the school.

Trouble at Home

Rumbling in the background of the young princes' time at Ludgrove were the problems that their parents were having in their marriage.

Discord had actually begun not long after the honeymoon, when Diana discovered that Charles still harboured affection for Camilla Parker Bowles. Charles, for his part, found that he didn't understand or know how to help his young wife with her insecurities and her difficulty adjusting to the stiffer, more ceremonial life as a senior royal. She had suffered from postnatal depression after William's birth and found it hard to cope with the rigours of being a royal. The couple had begun to live separate lives even before the official break-up and the princes spent some of their school holidays with their mother in London and some with their father at Highgrove.

The two boys only overlapped by a year in their time at Ludgrove because William was enrolled at Eton College, near Windsor in Berkshire, in 1995. That high-profile school had been the alma mater of many of Diana's male ancestors and contemporary family and had a much less spartan reputation than Charles' secondary school, Gordonstoun. When it came to their sons' education, arranging a gentler academic experience was something the royal couple could agree on.

Eton is well known for turning out many of the country's politicians and captains of industry. It used to be a place where the wealthy could apply for a place the moment their child was born, but that has changed over the past decades and now children have to pass entry exams and interviews and provide references.

While he was at Eton, William was elected to The Eton Society, reserved for elite prefects. Know affectionately as Pop, it derived from a debating society formed in 1811 and named Popina after the Latin for 'cook shop', the establishment where the students met to discuss matters of the day. Latterly, Pop members are expected to keep their younger fellow pupils in line and set a good example by their leadership qualities as well as helping out at school functions and parents' evenings. They are entitled to wear checked 'spongebag' trousers and a waistcoat of their own design.

Harry excelled at sport while at Eton, becoming a House Games Captain. Less academically minded, he opted for military academy after school, while William headed for university. ●

Prince Harry makes himself a piece of toast in the kitchen of his boarding house at Eton in 2003. (Tim Graham/Corbis/Getty Images)

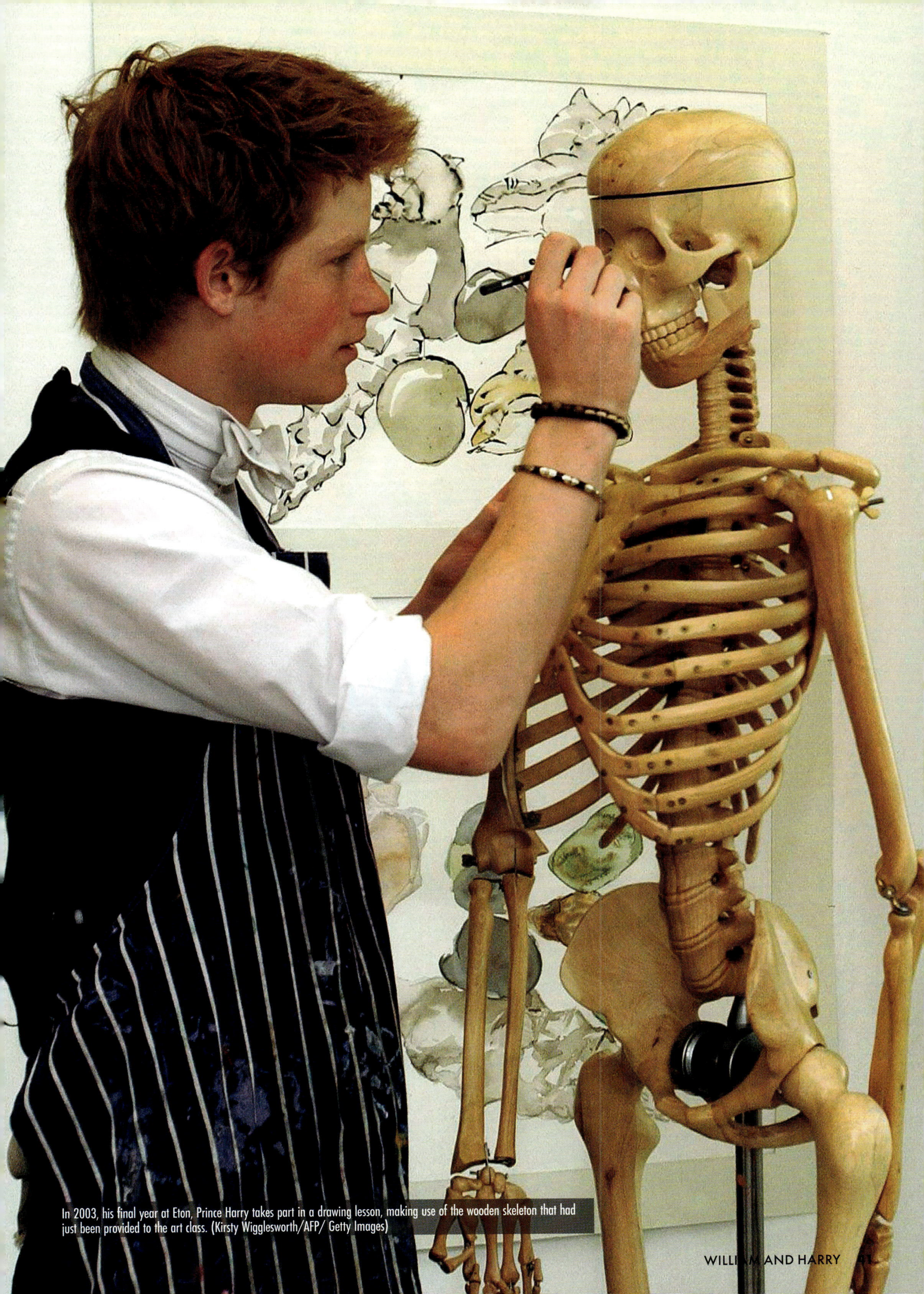

In 2003, his final year at Eton, Prince Harry takes part in a drawing lesson, making use of the wooden skeleton that had just been provided to the art class. (Kirsty Wigglesworth/AFP/ Getty Images)

YOUR ~~MA~~GAZINE

SAVE 18%
WHEN YOU SUBSCRIBE!

Aeroplane traces its lineage back to the weekly The Aeroplane launched in June 1911, and is still continuing to provide the best aviation coverage around. *Aeroplane* magazine is dedicated to offering the most in-depth and entertaining read on all historical aircraft.

shop.keypublishing.com/amsubs

Classic Land Rover is an exciting monthly magazine dedicated to Series and the classic Land Rovers. Written by enthusiasts, it is the complete guide to buying, owning, running, driving, repairing, modifying and restoring pre-nineties Land Rovers and Range Rover classics.

shop.keypublishing.com/clrsubs

ing.com

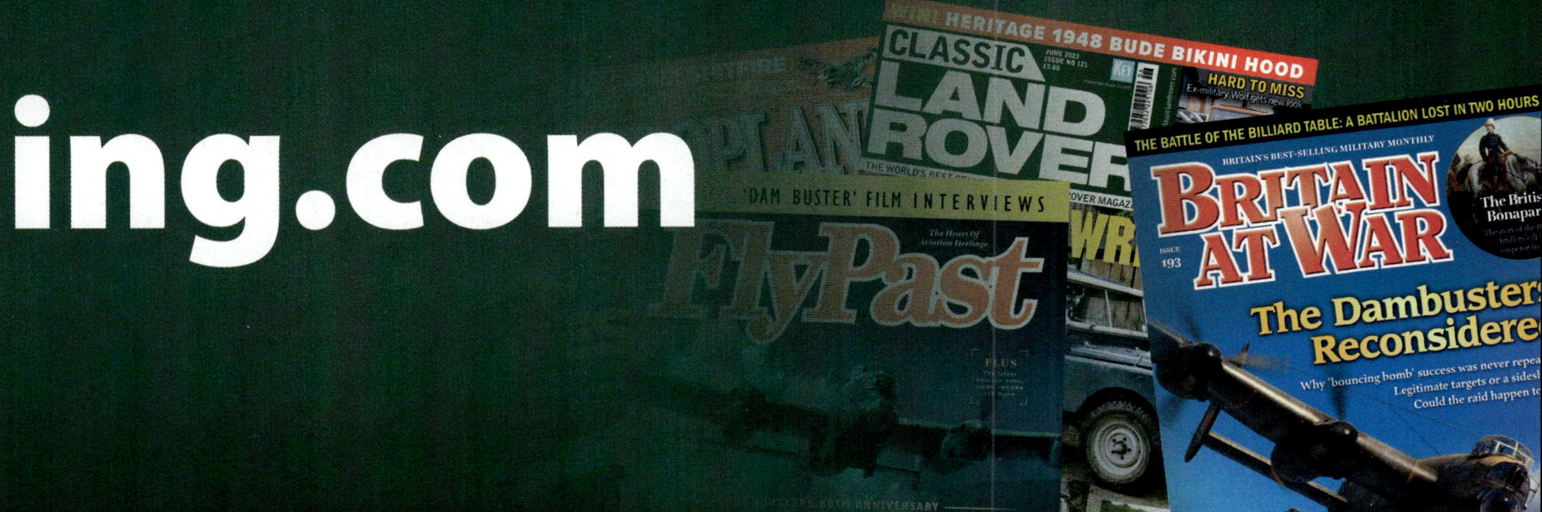

THE END OF A
MARRIAGE

The marriage of Prince Charles and Princess Diana began to break down publicly while their sons were still at school – an exceedingly difficult and emotional time for the two boys.

The relationship between the Prince and Princess of Wales had not been one built wholly on love but on duty and royal tradition. The births of their sons had brought them much joy but this was not sufficient to bind them closely together forever. They had different interests in life and an age gap that separated them culturally. Intense media interest since the announcement of their engagement had continued into the marriage and undermined Diana's peace of mind and security. The lack of privacy and the many official royal commitments the couple were expected to fulfil left them little time together to cement their relationship.

Not having been brought up in the discipline of a royal household, Diana found the requirements of life as the wife of the heir to the throne stifling. To always be at her husband's side at official engagements, to have bodyguards constantly with her, to be unable to do normal everyday activities without elaborate arrangements being made, even to go shopping or have lunch with a friend, were alien to her. The craving for normality increased even more with the birth of her sons. She suffered from terrible morning sickness and from post-natal depression, which further increased her vulnerability. Her own lack of parental support growing up, her parents' divorce, and the arrival of a stepmother she disliked, deprived her of a strong family prop to lean on.

For his part, those close to Prince Charles have said he found it difficult to understand his bride. He was so used to everything in his life being dictated by protocol and heritage, he couldn't appreciate how someone from outside that restricted circle could react to the boundaries that were such an accepted aspect of his life. In the prince's authorised biography written in 1994 by respected broadcaster Jonathan Dimbleby, The Queen was described as being "physically and emotionally distant"

Princess Diana's Personal Protection Officer Barry Mannakee with a three-year-old Prince William in 1985. Mannakee was rumoured to have had an affair with the princess and left her service a year later. (Tim Graham/Getty Images)

and Prince Philip as harsh and hectoring. Since childhood it had been instilled in Charles by his parents that his primary focus was to represent the Crown and the British people and that his personal interests and desires must always take second place. He had been moulded, shaped

and educated to eventually assume his role as monarch and head of the Commonwealth. This, naturally, interfered hugely with a normal family life, as it had with his parents before him.

Additionally, the biography revealed that Charles partially blamed his father for the

In the summer of 1991, the pretence that the royal marriage was intact was still the official line and like any other boy Prince Harry could enjoy his mother competing at his school sports day. (Tim Graham/Getty Images)

problems in his marriage, accusing him of having forced him into marrying a woman he hardly knew and didn't love for the sake of having someone who was acceptable to the establishment.

Ironically, according to her friends, after the births of the royal princes Diana began to see herself in a more positive light – not as the wife of a prince but as the mother of a future king. She had been embraced by the British public and the press began to court her as a style setter and young female role model that their readers responded to. Fashion designers wanted her to endorse their clothing and charities approached her to support their causes, knowing that her glamorous image would raise their profiles. Through all this she grew in confidence and an appreciation of her new position of influence.

A Love Rekindled

Gradually, the couple grew apart and began to look for companionship with people who could perhaps understand them better. For Charles this meant turning to a woman he had met and dated in the early 1970s, Camilla, now married to career soldier Andrew Parker Bowles, who was much closer to him in age than Diana. When they met, Camilla reportedly said to him: "My great grandmother was the mistress of your great great grandfather. I feel we have something in common." Their friendship had continued after their initial romantic association ended with Prince Charles going on active service with the Royal Navy between 1971 and 1976.

As a match, though, the relationship was not seen as ideal by the Palace, because Camilla had been born a Catholic. As contained in the Parliamentary Act of Settlement of 1701, anyone in the line of succession was barred from marrying a Catholic because of their perceived threat to the Crown. Following the end of the English Civil War, the Act was written to confirm that it was Parliament that had the right to determine who would reign and the Sovereign was bound to preserve the Anglican Church of England. Only the Protestant descendants of the granddaughter of King James I were deemed to be eligible to succeed to the monarchy and they

had to swear to defend the English church. The Act was finally superseded by the Succession to the Crown Act (2013), which also changed the system of male primogeniture, allowing a daughter to succeed to the crown before her brother, if she was the elder.

In the unfolding of Charles' personal life, by the time his stint with the navy had finished Camilla was married and shortly after that he was introduced to Diana. However, both of the Parker Bowles continued to be members of Charles' close circle of friends, with Andrew

being a member of the princes' polo team and Camilla sharing his love of art, books and classical music. She also joined him in riding, shooting and other country pursuits, many of the things Diana did not enjoy. Royal historian Marlene Koenig has written that the friends grew closer when Charles' beloved great uncle Earl Mountbatten was murdered by an IRA bomb in late 1979 and Camilla helped to comfort him, and that extreme closeness lasted until his engagement when they reverted to simply being good friends. ➲

Princess Diana with Captain James Hewitt and the boys at the Life Guards barracks in London. Hewitt had commissioned the regiment's tailors to make uniforms for the princes. (Anwar Hussein/Alamy Stock Photo)

In 1994, when being interviewed for a TV documentary called *Charles: The Private Man, the Public Role*, the prince responded to a question from interviewer Jonathan Dimbleby about whether he had been faithful to his wife by saying: "Yes, absolutely… until it became irretrievably broken down, both of us having tried." He also affirmed that a failure in his marriage was far from what he wanted. "I have always tried to get it right and tried to do the right thing by everybody." In saying that, he summed up the guiding principles of his life that he has tried to pass on to his sons. One television critic reviewed the programme's content by remarking that: "The headlines predictably zeroed in on the Prince's adultery and broad definition of faith, but 13 million viewers will have taken away a picture of a man as decent as he is troubled."

Diana's Indiscretions

Princess Diana's first affair was suspected of being with her personal bodyguard, Barry Mannakee, in 1985 when William was a toddler and Harry was just a year old. Although she never revealed his name, on a leaked video tape recorded by her voice coach in 1992 she did speak of someone she was deeply in love with: "who worked in this environment" and said she "would have been quite happy to give all this up and to just go off and live with him".

In 1986, Mannakee was transferred out of the Princess' service because his managers believed his relationship with his employer was inappropriate. He was later killed in a motorcycling accident, an incident that was to be the subject of extensive wild conspiracy theories that the security forces had been behind the accident, bolstered by the fact that Diana remarked in the original video: "I think he was bumped off, but there we are."

In 1986, Diana's five-year affair began with James Hewitt, a Captain in the Household Cavalry's Life Guards regiment. When they met, learning that he was a cavalry officer, Diana revealed that she was afraid of horses, having been thrown badly as a child. Prince Charles was keen that she try to ride again so that she could join him in a pastime he loved. Hewitt offered to give her lessons to help her overcome her fear and their relationship developed. Aside from occasions when Hewitt was allegedly smuggled into Kensington Palace, sometimes in the boot of a car, the couple's liaisons often took place at a cottage in Devon belonging to the Hewitt family. If Diana visited his family's home with her children, she was entertained by his mother while he took the boys riding. The man they called Uncle James also took them to his barracks to see the cavalry horses and some 'real-life' soldiers. He had khaki uniforms made for them by the regimental tailor and taught them how to drill.

When Hewitt was interviewed many years later by Australian television, he drew a picture of evenings in the country with Princess Diana that were more times of domestic bliss than wild passion. "I'd cook and she would wash up," he said. "Just dinner and relaxing and laughing." It injected an aspect of normal people's lives that was lacking in both Diana and the boys' royal existence. This was one of many interviews Hewitt has given about his time with the princess that have generated global headlines. He also participated in two 'tell-all' books and attempted to sell letters Diana wrote to him. This led to him being given the label 'Britain's biggest cad'.

Guests aboard Dodi Fayed's speedboat on a holiday in St Tropez in the south of France, just prior to the couple's tragic deaths in Paris in 1997. (Michel Dufour/WireImage)

In 1991 Hewitt was dispatched to serve in the Gulf War as a Challenger tank commander in Operation Desert Storm, despite Diana's protestations and offers to speak to his commanding officer, and the affair ended. The publication three years later of the book with which he collaborated, called *Princess in Love*, was seen by the princes as a horrible betrayal on the part of Uncle James. Then 12 and ten years old, they must have felt acutely the embarrassment dealt to their mother and father, even though their parents had by that time been separated for two years.

Further Embarrassment

At the same time as her affair with James Hewitt, Diana's name was linked to another man's – James Gilbey, the heir to the gin-making family. He was the person on the other end of the line when Diana's phone call was purportedly taped by a radio ham using his frequency scanning equipment. A transcript of the recording made it into newsprint, publicising that she had a long conversation with someone – not her husband – who repeatedly called her Squidge or Squidgy and talked about holding her close. An affair was denied by both parties and the matter settled into just a frank and confidential conversation between two old friends.

The taping of the phone call was, however, viewed more seriously, as its appearance was coincident on a recording of a highly personal call between the Prince of Wales and Camilla Parker Bowles. The existence of both eventually pointed to the phone tapping and covert surveillance of celebrities that went on to assume such notoriety within tabloid press circles.

In 1992, journalist and biographer Andrew Morton published a book entitled *Diana: Her True Story*. Some years previously, James Colthurst, a radiologist at London's St Thomas' Hospital and a friend of Diana's from the days when she was a nanny, had met Morton at a press event to unveil a new CT scanner for his department. The year before the book was released Colthurst allegedly became an intermediary between the princess and the writer, taping her answers to Morton's questions that would form the substance of the book.

The justification for the book was, according to Colthurst in a later television documentary interview, the actions of the anonymous string-pullers at the Palace. "There was a great deal of jealousy from the grey men who sat behind Prince Charles, not wanting him to be living in her shadow. Her character was being written down – as she saw it, a campaign to sideline her and remove her from the boys. That was her worry, that she was going to lose the boys – overriding, above everything else, that was the concern – and that they were using a character

run-down as a means of making that happen, an understandable next step." It's not known if that fear was communicated to the boys, but there must have been an atmosphere around them of uncertainty in the future.

Just before the publication Diana wrote to Colthurst: "Obviously we are preparing for the volcano to erupt and I do feel better equipped to cope with whatever comes our way! Thank you for your belief in me and for taking the trouble to understand this mind – it's such a relief not to be on my own anymore and that it's okay to be me." Colthurst later shared his thoughts on Diana's legacy in a newspaper interview. "She set a high bar for her sons, who have both inherited her natural way with others. Both have her sensitivity and caring. But they are also gutsy and tough and share their mother's passion for using their roles to do good in the world."

A legal separation for the Prince and Princess of Wales followed the publication of the book and this was the situation for the next three years until Diana's now notorious interview with journalist Martin Bashir for the BBC's *Panorama* series at the end of 1995. Later proved to have been obtained by deception, the interview had an explosive effect, laying bare the couple's relationship, including Diana's own affairs and her husband's with Camilla Parker Bowles, and culminating in the oft-quoted phrase "there were three of us in this marriage, so it was a bit crowded".

This was a very public exposure of their broken family life for the princes, then just 13 and 11 years old.

The Divorce

Eventually, The Queen herself encouraged Prince Charles to divorce his wife, sensing that the situation was never going to be repaired and hoping that divorce would dampen down the fever of press interest. But the divorce itself did not go through smoothly, setting precedents as it was bound to do, and further involved the two young princes in their parents' unhappiness. Just prior to the divorce becoming final Diana wrote to one of her close friends, Susie Kassem, saying: "I am having a very difficult time and the pressure is serious and coming from all sides. It's too difficult sometimes to keep one's head up and today I'm on my knees and just longing for this divorce to go through as the possible cost is tremendous."

A month later she wrote again: "If I had known a year ago what I'd experience going through this divorce, I'd never have consented – it's desperate and ugly."

At the time that her divorce was announced, Diana was in the middle of a two-year affair with heart and lung surgeon Hasnat Khan, a man she called Mr Wonderful. They met when Diana was with a friend in Royal Brompton Hospital waiting to hear the results of heart surgery on the friend's husband. The surgeon who came out to talk to them was Khan and after that meeting they ran into each other again when she paid her friend repeat visits. They began dating, going to jazz clubs or getting takeaways to eat at Kensington Palace to avoid being seen in public at restaurants.

Khan was introduced to William and Harry and the couple apparently discussed marriage after Diana's divorce but the worries he had about press intrusion and the fact that a normal life would be impossible because of it led them to parting company a month before she died. Khan tried to call Diana on the night of her death and in a police interview he gave after the accident he said: "My main concern about us getting married was that my life would be hell because of who she was. I knew I would not be able to live a normal life and if we ever had children together, I would not be able to take them anywhere or do normal things with them." Ironically, he was exactly describing the life experienced by Diana's existing sons.

Diana's final fling was with Dodi Fayed, the son of Harrods owner Mohamed Al-Fayed, who she had met at a polo match in Windsor as far back as 1986. He hosted a holiday from St Tropez ➲

Prince Charles and the Duchess of Cornwall visiting Salisbury in 2018 to boost morale following the poisoning of former Soviet agent Sergei Skripal and his daughter. (Simon Ward Photography/Shutterstock)

in the south of France to Sardinia for her and the two boys before the couple then flew to Paris where they were involved in the fatal car crash.

Welcoming a Stepmother

Following Diana's death, Prince Charles' greatest desire was to marry his youthful sweetheart who had been a friend and support to him for so many years. But he was aware that there were huge obstacles to overcome – the feelings of his two bereaved sons, public opinion, The Queen's disapproval and the Church of England rules on anyone in the line to the throne marrying a divorcée. The last of these considerations was not something to be taken lightly. In 1992, Princess Anne remarried in Scotland to sidestep that Anglican edict.

According to his authorised biography, written by broadcaster Jonathan Dimbleby, Prince Charles had rekindled his relationship with Camilla in 1986, the same year Diana began her affair with James Hewitt. He had hosted a 50th birthday party for her at Highgrove a couple of months before Diana's fatal car accident, as part of a campaign to introduce Camilla to the British public as his partner. These moves were put into abeyance during the mourning period but in 1998 it was reported that Prince William had been formally introduced to his father's friend and the following year they made their first public appearance as a couple and went on holiday together with William and Harry.

In 2000, The Queen signalled she had given her official approval of her son's relationship, but it was another two years before they moved into Clarence House together, the Prince's official London residence. In February 2005 the couple announced their engagement and in April of that year they were married at the Windsor Guildhall, a private hire venue in the centre of the Berkshire town. Although The Queen was not present at the wedding, she attended the reception.

Having originally been opposed to their father remarrying, fearing yet another media circus and Camilla being compared to their mother, the two princes did come round when they saw how much happiness she was bringing to his life.

Prince Harry listens attentively to his stepmother Camilla on the balcony of Buckingham Palace during the Trooping the Colour ceremony in 2015. (Chris Jackson/Getty Images)

In his memoir Prince Harry remembered when they announced they were to be married. "We recognised that he was finally going to be with the woman he loved, the woman he'd always loved, the woman Fate might've intended for him in the first place. Whatever bitterness or sorrow we felt over the closing of another loop in Mummy's story, we understood that it was beside the point... I wanted so many things, but I was surprised to discover at their wedding that one of the things I wanted most was for my father to be happy." ●

Prince William and Camilla share the enjoyment of the Platinum Jubilee pageant which celebrated The Queen's 70 years on the throne in 2022. (Mark Cuthbert/Getty Images)

Princess Diana's coffin is carried into Westminster Abbey where the bearers pause before the tomb of the Unknown Warrior. The two young princes stand side by side, united in their grief but prohibited by royal convention from comforting each other. (Ken Goff/Getty Images)

DEATH OF A MOTHER

One of the most traumatic events that can happen in a young child's life is the death of a parent. For William and Harry, their mother's passing was accompanied by what seemed like an entire nation in very demonstrative mourning and a worldwide media circus.

A 19-year-old Diana in 1980, already pursued by members of the press eager to hear whether an engagement to Prince Charles was about to be announced. (John Minihan/Getty Images)

prince and part of a system that discouraged a public show of emotion had its most devastating effect. Never has the world-renowned British stiff-upper-lip been more in evidence. The traditions of centuries of royal lines came into play when it was suggested that the princes should walk behind their mother's coffin from St James' Palace as the cortege made its way from Kensington Palace to Westminster Abbey for the funeral service.

In this unprecedented situation, no one was certain of protocol, especially when it came to two young, bereaved boys, and Diana's brother, Earl Spencer, was critical of any move to require William and Harry to play a very public role in the funeral. The pressure came from government and the royal household, concerned that if Prince Charles alone accompanied the cortege he could have been open to verbal and even possibly physical attacks from the onlookers, who blamed him for the break-up of his marriage and, by association, for Diana's death.

Eventually, their grandfather, Prince Philip, offered that if the boys would walk, he would walk and so they did, flanked by Prince Charles and their uncle Charles Spencer. William later said that it was one of the hardest things he had ever had to do but that he felt it was right ➲

The aftermath of the accident that took the life of Princess Diana and robbed the two young princes of her unconditional love and support, was a circumstance no teenager could survive unscathed. In fact, Prince Harry was two weeks short of his 13th birthday when the car carrying his mother collided with a concrete pillar in a Parisian underpass. He and Prince William were on holiday with The Queen, Prince Philip and Prince Charles at Balmoral when the call came through that shattered their lives.

In his autobiography Harry recalled his father waking him in the night, telling him the news. "He sat down on the edge of the bed. He put a hand on my knee. 'Darling boy, Mummy's been in a car crash'... I remember waiting patiently for Pa to confirm that Mummy was all right. And I remember him not doing that."

Prince Charles wanted to shield his sons from the media spotlight that he knew would shine bright, and for a while that was possible. Eventually, however, he and the boys would have to return to London for all the formalities and the funeral. This was when being a royal

The Prince and Princess of Wales with William and Harry in happier times for the children, 10 years before her tragic death. (Tim Graham/Getty Images)

The overwhelming sight of floral tributes to their mother, an experience that Harry in particular found hard to deal with, despite the company of his father and brother. (Tim Graham/Getty Images)

Prince Philip, Prince William, Earl Spencer, Prince Harry and Prince Charles follow Princess Diana's funeral procession in a solemn line on September 6, 1997. (Jeff J Mitchell/Getty Images)

because it was a "balance between duty and family". At the age of 15, this demonstrated how ingrained the sense of duty had become, a reflection of what would carry him on as heir to the throne.

Coping With it All

Harry's focus on that emotional day was to be a support to his brother. He said that if roles had been reversed William would not have let him walk alone, so he was glad to be there. "I remember feeling numb. I remember clenching my fists. I remember keeping a fraction of Willy always in the corner of my vision and drawing loads of strength from that. Most of all I remember the sounds, the clinking bridles and clopping hooves of the six sweaty horses, the squeaking wheels of the gun carriage they were hauling... they were in such sharp contrast to the otherwise all-encompassing silence... The only hint that we were marching through a canyon of humanity was the occasional wail."

The lasting effect of their mother's death on boys as young as they were, however, was revealed in an interview Prince Harry later gave when he said: "I can safely say that losing my mum at the age of 12, and therefore shutting down all of my emotions for the last

The eternal flame sculpture in Paris that sits over the underpass in which Diana died, has become an unofficial monument to the princess. (Demerzel21/dreamstime.com)

Princes William and Harry, with their uncle Charles Spencer, listening to the Dean of Westminster after the funeral. (Princess Diana Archive/Getty Images)

20 years, has had a quite serious effect on not only my personal life but my work as well. I have probably been very close to a complete breakdown on numerous occasions."

Over the years, however, he has found that not bottling up his emotions has had a positive impact on his mental health. "The experience I have had is that once you start talking about it, you realise that actually you're part of quite a big club," he has said. His goal in joining with his brother to set up a charity called Heads Together in 2017 was, "to normalize the conversation to the point where anyone can sit down and have

a coffee and just go 'you know what, I've had a really bad day, can I just tell about it?' Because then you walk away and it's done."

Although he has not been as publicly vocal about it, Prince William did echo his brother's sentiments in a broadcast conversation with singer Lady Gaga as part of the Head Together charity's #oktosay campaign. "It's time that everyone speaks up," he said. "Just having a conversation with a friend or family member can really make such a difference. It's OK to have this conversation. It's really important to have this conversation." ●

The two young princes bow their heads as the coffin containing their mother is taken from Westminster Abbey following her funeral service in 1997. (Adam Butler/AFP/Getty Images)

In an unprecedented outpouring of public regret at Princess Diana's death, flowers, messages, photographs and patriotic tributes have been hung on the Kensington Palace gates each year on the anniversary of the accident. (Alessandro Abbonizio/AFP/Getty Images)

OUT INTO THE WORLD

School days behind them, the princes graduated into a patchwork life where official duties, pomp and ceremony had to be navigated alongside existing in a real world with ordinary people.

On the first leg of his gap year, in Chile in South America in 2000, Prince William carries a large tree trunk to be used in the construction of a walkway to link buildings in the village of Tortel. (Tim Graham/Corbis/Getty Images)

In modern times, the country expects its royals to be accessible and to demonstrate their human sides. However, they are not expected to court controversy, have strong opinions, make mistakes, or reveal their feet of clay. It is a tricky path to follow, especially when there are camera lenses trained on just about every public move. The media frenzy that had begun with Princess Diana and the salacious details of the Prince and Princess of Wales' marital problems had little abated. No longer was there the respect shown to royals in previous generations, with the slight exception of The Queen, although she had suffered more than a little in the aftermath of Diana's death.

So, in an effort to ease his sons into a world that was poised to trip them up, Prince Charles and his team continued their negotiations with the press and their trade-off of cooperation in return for a guarantee of at least some privacy for the boys. The other consideration was the effect of a royal media circus on the princes' contemporaries in further education. To an extent, when the boys were at school they were associating with children whose parents were equally high-

Prince William enjoys a spot of skiing in Switzerland with Prince Charles during an Easter university break, wearing a copper bracelet he got in Africa on the second leg of his gap year. (Tim Graham/Getty Images)

profile in their own fields – heads of companies, politicians, foreign dignitaries. At university and in military training the students and recruits came from a vast range of backgrounds and family incomes. To expose them to the information-gathering, photo-seeking subterfuge that surrounded the royals was not only to be unfair to them but also to set up the princes as 'different', people who had to be treated with caution and not befriended naturally.

This horse trading with the media was evident in the handling of William's first days at the University of St Andrews in the famous Scottish golfing town. Instead of attending Freshers' Week with the other students, he arrived at his halls of residence a few days later, at the end of a royal visit with his father to Glasgow and Edinburgh. A lot of the townspeople were there to see him, along with the usual coterie of members of the press. Photographs over, that was supposed to be the end of the intrusion. The press had agreed to leave the prince alone to settle into his new environment. In general, the arrangement was that neither William nor Harry would be photographed throughout their terms of full-time education without their consent.

By and large this agreement held, for a while anyway, spoilt in the beginning only by the arrival in William's first week of a camera crew making a documentary series, *Royalty A-Z*, for American TV. They claimed they had permission, not from Colleen Harris, then Prince Charles' Press Secretary, but from Prince Edward, William's uncle and owner of the film company. An embarrassing furore ensued that saw Prince Edward returning swiftly from holiday to proffer effusive apologies.

Gap Year and Student Life

After leaving Eton in 2000, like many other young people, Prince William decided to take a gap year. He joined the Welsh Guards on an exercise in Belize, travelled through Africa – Kenya, Tanzania, Botswana and the island of Rodrigues – and then went to the village of Tortel in Chile, South America, with expedition organiser Raleigh International. There he worked on constructions to help the villagers and taught English. The houses in Tortel are largely built on stilts as the area covers a number of islands with channels between them, requiring wooden walkways made from the plentiful local timber for getting around rather than conventional streets.

After his gap year, like any first-time student, Prince William must have been a little apprehensive starting his first term. Unlike most of his contemporaries, he was striking out without a lot of his accustomed support system. Only his PPOs were there. In all other respects he was setting up in his room in halls and having to get used to living with other students without an army of servants to cater for him. His allocated room was in St Salvator's Hall, nicknamed Sallies, where accommodation was arranged along corridors with shared showers and bathrooms, a dining hall and kitchen

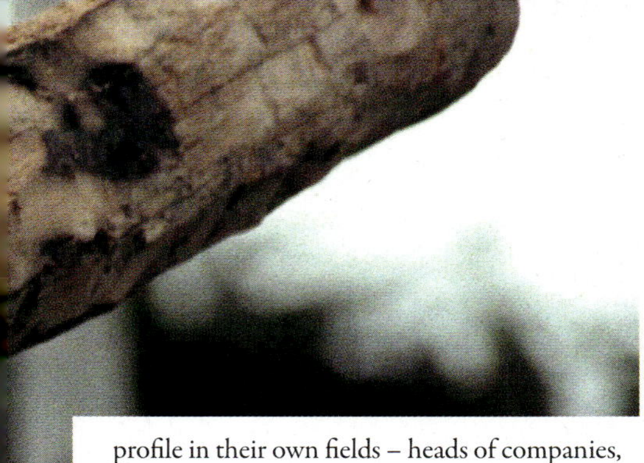

Prince Harry on his gap year in Lesotho in 2004, planting a peach tree in the gardens of Mants'ase Children's Home with four-year-old Mutsu Potsane, who would become an important part of his life. (John Stillwell/AFP via Getty Images)

facilities for making snacks, common rooms, a library, a laundry and a computer room.

University life was an opportunity for the prince to behave like everyone else, not be singled out because of his lineage; take the rough with the smooth, mix with people from a wide variety of backgrounds and learn about their lives. Study, sport and going out for drinks and meals with friends occupied his time… and meeting girls, notably one girl.

Catherine Middleton lived in the same halls of residence in their first year and the following year they moved into a shared house with a group of other student friends. The two were delighted to discover that they had something in common – they had both worked on the Raleigh project in Chile, although not at the same time. Nevertheless, they had met and laboured alongside the same expedition organisers and village people, so they instantly bonded.

The prince's geography lecturer praised his efforts to be just another one of the 7,500

As part of his experiences immediately after university, Prince William took part in exercises with the Royal Air Force Mountain Rescue service in Anglesey, Wales at the end of 2005. (Max Mumby/Getty Images)

students at St Andrews. "He tried as hard as he could to experience a normal student programme and he did a very good job of that. I'm amazed that he managed to stay focused with all the obvious attention. He managed to stay focused for four years and keep his head down and get some work done."

David Corner, the university's Secretary and Registrar, was in charge of student welfare at the time Prince William was studying there. He tried to help the young prince navigate a world where his royal-ness set him apart. "He was the sort of student who was never going to get into academic difficulty, a student who was conscientious. What I noticed as an outsider was this tremendous thing that I suspect most members of the royal family have, which is a notion of obedience, a notion that you do what you're told."

Australia and Africa

After school Prince Harry took a gap year like his older brother but whereas William went to Chile, Harry set off for a few months working in the Australian outback. Royal bodyguard Mark Dyer arranged his stay with a former flatmate of Princess Diana's, now married to an Australian cattle farmer. Harry's placement would be as a jackaroo, or farm hand. It was a completely different experience to his life so far. "Tooloombilla… was like no place I'd ever been," he said in his autobiography. "I came from a green place. The Hills' farm was an ode to brown. I came from a place where every move was monitored, catalogued, and subjected to judgement. The Hills's farm was so vast and remote that no one would see me for most of the day but George [the Hills' eldest son and Harry's mentor for the stay]. And the odd wallaby."

Unfortunately, Harry's stint on the farm coincided with the publication of the memoirs of Princess Diana's former butler, Paul Burrell. This reignited the press interest in how the princes were coping with their mother's death and sparked sensational revelations about her life in the royal family. So, remote as the Australian farm was, photographers found their way there. It was deemed to be time for Harry to move on. "I owed so much to the Hills," he said. "I didn't want to repay them by ruining their lives. I didn't want to be the cause of them losing the one resource more precious than water – privacy. I thanked them for nine of the best weeks of my life and flew home…"

Prince William with his father and stepmother as he leaves his graduation at the University of St Andrews in 2005, holding his MA (Hons) degree in Geography certificate. (Tim Graham/Getty Images)

Next stop for Harry was the southern African country of Lesotho where the population had been ravaged by the spread of HIV and the Aids epidemic. This post-school experience had a profound effect on the young prince, bringing him into contact with so many children who had lost everything – parents and homes. "Poverty, disease, orphans – death. It rendered everything else rubbish," he said. "In Lesotho, no matter what you were going through, you were well-off compared to others."

His experience in Lesotho led Prince Harry to set up the Sentebale charity with the son of the king, Prince Seeiso, to give opportunities to the country's most disadvantaged children. It is a relationship that has continued over the past two decades, as has Harry's friendship with the small child he met in his gap year there, Mutsu Potsane, who grew up to work at the orphanage, met the prince many times and was invited to Harry and Meghan's wedding.

The next stage in Harry's life was training at the famous Sandhurst Military School that has turned out generations of army officers. He joined in 2005, slightly before his brother, who was finishing his university degree before embarking on a military life. ●

Family friend Hugh van Cutsem, Prince Harry and Prince William share a joke at a formal event in Chester, Cheshire in 2004. (Max Mumby/Indigo/Getty Images)

THE SUPPORT OF
FRIENDS

At school, in further education and beyond, William and Harry have made close friends who have kept their secrets and supported them through thick and thin.

Shared experiences in the classroom and on the playing field forged alliances with friends whose loyalty protected the princes from press intrusion over some of their youthful indiscretions and the trauma of their mother's death. Later in their lives their friends have guarded the privacy of their personal relationships with girlfriends and then wives. They have pledged to safeguard their children and have supported them in their aims in life.

Not all of the friends survived to join the princes' circles in adult life, however. One such was Henry van Straubenzee who died in a car accident when he was only 18 years old. One of Harry's closest friends from junior school, he was nicknamed Henners by the prince. He wrote of him with affection in his memoir *Spare*, relating some of the hijinks they got up to together, such as stealing strawberries and mooning at the school security cameras. The Straubenzee family had three boys – Thomas, Nicholas and

Henry – who were all friends with the young royals. Nicolas is godfather to William's son Prince Louis, while the oldest, Thomas, is godfather to his daughter, Princess Charlotte. Thomas was also an usher at William and Kate's wedding and formed a double act with William's old Etonian friend James Meade to share humorous anecdotes about the groom at the reception.

A while after Henry Straubenzee's death his family set up a foundation in his memory that raises money for education in Uganda to fight

Some of the princes' closest friends attending a wedding in 2013 – (left to right) Harry Aubrey-Fletcher, Thomas van Straubenzee, Guy Pelly and Tom Inskip. (Max Mumby/Indigo/Getty Images)

Left to right: Hugh Grosvenor, Duke of Westminster, Jake Warren, Charlie van Straubenzee and Arthur Landon arrive for Prince Harry's wedding in 2018. (Max Mumby/Getty Images)

The arm of childhood friend Harry Aubrey-Fletcher reaches round two other spectators to tweak Prince William's ear and catch his attention at Cheltenham Races in 2013, demonstrating how close a chum he is to the prince. (Max Mumby/Indigo/Getty Images)

Prince Harry and his teammate Nacho Figueras at Polo Cup match in Aspen, Colorado in 2022. The two close friends play at the Santa Barbara Polo and Racquets Club in California. (Chris Jackson/Getty Images)

Prince Harry looks sad and reflective at the 2009 launch of the Henry van Straubenzee Memorial Fund for his best friend from school who was killed in a car accident in 2002. (Toby Melville/AFP via Getty Images)

From Childhood Onwards

Prince William, in return, is godfather to Grace, the daughter of the fourth van Cutsem brother, Hugh Jr. She became famous at the age of only three when she was the bridesmaid at William and Kate's wedding and was seen on Buckingham Palace balcony scowling and with her hands over her ears as the couple shared their first public kiss.

School friend James Meade and Oliver Baker, a university friend of both William and Kate, were also invited to be godparents to the couple's children. Prince Louis counts Harry Aubrey-Fletcher, another friend of William's from Eton, as one of his godfathers, as well as Guy Pelly, a friend since childhood of both William and Harry. Pelly lived near them in Sandringham and was one of the crowd of friends they invited to the Club H cellar room at Highgrove House and the local pubs when they were teenagers. In Pelly's case, although he was very discreet about the activities of the princes in their drinking days, he was considered to be a bad influence by Prince Charles, who was not keen for them to spend time together in their youth. This reservation about the suitability of the mischievous Pelly as a companion was borne out by the trouble Harry later got into at a fancy dress party organised by James Meade when he was photographed dressed as a Nazi alongside Pelly dressed as The Queen.

Pelly went on to run a string of high-end nightclubs in London's Mayfair district that the princes frequented in their young adulthood. He now owns a vineyard in the state of Virginia, USA but has stayed in touch with the princes, hosting them both at his wedding in 2016.

Catherine Middleton and Oliver Baker have a relaxing day at Cheltenham racecourse in 2007. The pair had become good friends with Prince William at St Andrews University. (Max Mumby/Indigo/Getty Images)

poverty. Like Harry, Henry spent part of his gap year after school in Africa, in his case Uganda, and his legacy has been a charity that supports 51 schools there with teaching resources and funding building repairs.

The van Cutsem family is another dynasty that has been friendly with Prince Charles since he and the elder Hugh met at Cambridge University. His oldest son, Edward, was a page boy at Charles and Diana's wedding and two of the other brothers, William and Nicholas, have stood as godparents to William's children. The van Cutsems took William and Harry to Lewa Game Reserve in Kenya as part of the strategy to get them away from the furore in the UK after their mother was killed. They would often have them to stay at the family home in the country to help them get over their bereavement. The family originally rented Anmer Hall in Norfolk, which later became the first marital home of William and Catherine.

Prince Harry has shared all of these friends with his brother over the years as they all eventually formed part of the same social circles as adults. Having moved to the United States, he has formed a new group of close friends, including filmmaker Tyler Perry. He lent Harry and Meghan his house in Los Angeles as a safe place to stay after they had left Britain and while they organised a home of their own in Montecito, California.

Another person who has made a difference in Harry's life is Argentinian polo player, Nacho Figueras. He formed a polo four at the Santa Barbara Polo and Racquets Club and invited Harry to join them. He now practises there weekly and plays regularly with his Los Padres team, named after the National Forest in the hills behind Santa Barbara. ●

THIS
SPORTING LIFE

Both brothers have excelled at sport throughout their lives, notably on the polo field. A common love of outdoor activity bonded the two boys for much of their youth.

All the schools Princes William and Harry attended lay emphasis on the playing of sport – for health reasons and for the benefits to other areas of the students' lives that comes from the discipline required to play well. Pastimes such as skiing also reinforced relations between the boys and their parents and gave them precious leisure time away from royal duties and prying lenses. In order to ensure that they had time to themselves, every year they took to the slopes the holiday proper would be preceded by a photocall. This cooperation with the press was on the understanding that photographers would then leave them alone to enjoy their skiing without attempting to capture their every move.

While he was at Ludgrove School, William was in the hockey team. In fact, at the age of nine he met his future bride on the playing field. She was in her school team and they had arranged a match with Ludgrove. Much more recently the couple demonstrated that they hadn't forgotten the skills of the game when they made a four-day trip to Sweden and Norway in 2018 and competed in a best-of-three penalty shoot-out playing bandy hockey on an outdoor ice rink.

Harry's game at school was rugby. He was House Games Captain and took part in competitive inter-house matches as well as those with other school teams. His position as a royal prince did lead to some tough times from his schoolmates as he related in a 2016 documentary on rugby playing called *Beyond the Tryline*. "People would see me on the rugby field as an opportunity to smash me up and actually there was people in my own school during inter-house rugby competitions that would beat me up... not beat me up exactly, but basically put in bigger tackles because it was me."

Believing in the power of sport to give young people confidence and life skills, he went on to spend part of his gap year after school training as an Assistant Development Officer with the Rugby Football Union. He then took his qualifications out to schools and clubs to help community coaches teach the game to children from a wide range of backgrounds, attempting to dispel the notion of it as a 'toffs' game. He followed this up in 2013 by becoming patron of the Rugby Football Union's All Schools Programme, promoting the game and improving junior facilities around the country.

At school and university William also enjoyed playing rugby, although the potential for injury must have given the Palace cause for concern as he is in the direct line to the throne. In fact, the worst that happened was a broken finger that required surgery while he was playing at Eton. By contrast, his brother Harry had his nose broken colliding with a goal post at the age of 16, also during an Eton game, and he broke a thumb and sustained shoulder damage when he was caught in a hard tackle.

Winter sports have always been a favourite of both princes, and family holidays to Klosters in Switzerland a regular event, as seen here in 1995 as they pose for the cameras with their sledges. (Tim Graham/Getty Images)

Accomplished bikers William and Harry take part in the gruelling 1,000-mile off-road dirt bike rally across South Africa to raise money for charity in 2008. (Tim Graham/Getty Images)

At St Andrew's university William was Captain of the water polo team, competing in 2004 in the Scottish National Universities' side at an international competition against Wales in Cardiff. "He gave as good as he got," said the Welsh Universities team captain Oliver Newcombe, who had warned the prince that he risked losing his good looks during the game. "We didn't single him out for any special treatment. Water polo is a hard sport to play – it's sort of rugby in the water. He played pretty well, I think. The standard this year was very hard."

William has been known to enjoy surfing and he succeeded his father as Patron of the British Sub Aqua Club. When they were old enough to hold a licence, both William and Harry took up motorcycling, although it was not an activity ➲

Prince Harry in 2001 playing for the Oppidans team at the traditional Eton Wall Game – a rough blend of football and rugby – played exclusively at the Berkshire school. (Tim Graham/Getty Images)

William and Harry chat together companionably having competed in a polo trophy match at Cirencester Park Polo Club in Gloucestershire in 2013. (Anwar Hussein/WireImage)

Tomlinson took a very practical stance with the two princes. They already knew how to ride when they first went to her for lessons; her job was to improve those skills to competition level. Prince William joined her first. He was the same age as her son Mark and the two boys formed a lasting friendship. "We did a lot of riding and jumping and having fun," said Tomlinson of the prince. "He's very competitive but if you're going to play a sport you might as well be competitive. And he's analytical about his own performance; he doesn't like playing badly. So many people who ride treat their horses like machines, but he has never done that – he treats a horse like a living being which has limits, but he will get the best out of it."

The two princes' contrasting styles were described by polo champion Malcolm Borwick, who has played in many tournaments with them. "Polo is often a reflection of your personality. ➲

that filled their parents and grandparents with joy. Their competence, however, led in 2008 to an eight-day, 1,000-mile off-road dirt bike rally across South Africa to raise money for the charity Prince Harry founded, Sentebale, and also Unicef and the Nelson Mandela Children's Fund. Before they set off Prince William said: "It's a great way of bringing all the three charities together and understanding the fact that Aids in Africa is still a major issue."

Since their lives had taken different paths after graduating from Sandhurst Military Academy two years previously, the brothers had not had many occasions to be together for any length of time. "We never really spend any time together – we've got separate jobs going on at the moment," said Prince Harry in a BBC interview before the event. "But it's great fun – well I don't know yet, we'll have to tell you. We might argue, we might have a bit of fun. It's not just a bimble across the countryside that's for sure, it's going to be very challenging and we're expecting to fall off many a time." Commenting on what would be raised for charity and Harry's assertion that eight days together would be fun, Prince William quipped: "The pain of spending a week with my brother is well worth it."

United by Polo

While both princes enjoyed playing rugby and football with their contemporaries in education and the military, it was a huge enjoyment of polo that united them as brothers on the same playing field. Polo teams only consist of four mounted players so whether they were taking part on the same team or a rival one, the contact has always been close and personal. Their camaraderie shone out in pictures taken at the many games they played together. Apart from the enjoyment they got out of riding and competing and maintaining their physical fitness, they also used their ability at the sport as a means to raise a lot of money for their charities.

Both princes were taught to play polo by Claire Tomlinson, who was the country's highest-rated female polo player and captain and then coach of the English national team. She was the first woman to compete against men at the top level – so rare were female competitors at the time she joined her university team in 1964, she had to be registered for matches as Mr Lucas. With her husband Simon she ran the Beaufort Polo Club in Gloucestershire, situated near to Highgrove House.

The game of polo has always brought the two princes together, enjoying a sport they both love and at which they excel. (Max Mumby/Indigo/Getty Images)

The brother compete on opposite sides in a charity polo match in 2013 at the Beaufort Polo Club in Gloucestershire where they both learned to play. (Anwar Hussein/WireImage)

The princes brave the cold to play for the local Black Horse pub team in the annual charity Sandringham football match at King's Lynn, Norfolk in 2015, winning 4-1. (Danny E Martindale/GC Images)

Prince Harry is by nature very optimistic as a person and always pushing boundaries, always challenging people, and that's how he plays polo. The Duke of Cambridge, Prince William, is a defensive player – he's very controlled, and plays really well in his role in the back."

While Prince William's polo-playing days are limited now by his family commitments and royal duties, and mainly confined to charity events, Prince Harry has taken the sport to a professional level since he moved to live full-time in California. He plays for the Los Padres team based at the Santa Barbara Polo and Racquets Club and trains there several times a week. His teammate is the Argentinian Nacho Figueros, the founder of the Californian club, with whom he has formed a close bond.

Keen Spectators Too

Apart from taking part in these activities, both brothers also love watching sport. In William's case this is particularly rugby, which is a passion he also shares with his wife. He has been the Royal Patron of the Welsh Rugby Union since 2016, having previously been Vice Royal Patron from 2007. Six years after that he became Patron of the Welsh Rugby Charitable Trust. Meanwhile, Kate was made Patron of both the English Rugby Football Union and League in 2022, roles she inherited from Prince Harry when he left the UK. Their allegiances understandably clash when they attend Wales v England matches, as they did early in 2023 for a Six Nations fixture in Cardiff, but their rivalry is always good humoured.

Football is another big area of interest for Prince William. He is a keen supporter of the Birmingham club Aston Villa. He has supported them since 2000 when, at the age of 18, he went with friends to his first FA Cup game, Bolton v Aston Villa, at the latter's home ground, Villa Park. He is quoted as saying: "All my friends

During the Commonwealth Games in Glasgow in 2014 the princes share a light-hearted moment watching the Wales v Scotland hockey match. (Max Mumby/Indigo/Getty Images)

at school were either Manchester United or Chelsea fans… I wanted to have a team that was more mid-table, that could give me more emotional rollercoaster moments. It was fantastic, I sat with all the Brummie fans with my red beanie on and had a great time. It was the atmosphere, the camaraderie and I really felt that there was something I could connect with."

William went on to become President of the Football Association and to crystallise his feeling about the power of football to unite people when he said: "At its best, football is a powerful force for good in society. It binds people from different backgrounds, communities, faiths and abilities and gives them a common interest, a unifying identity."

For his part, since his move to the United States Harry has embraced the sports of baseball and American football, appearing with his wife at games and taking part in promotional events. ●

Prince Harry looks askance at his brother's raucous support of his team at the 2015 England v Wales Rugby World Cup match at Twickenham Stadium in London. (Max Mumby/Indigo/Getty Images)

The two princes enjoy a chat at Sandhurst Military Academy in Surrey in 2006. (Tim Graham/Getty Images)

A FORCE FOR GOOD

Following in the footsteps of their father, grandfather and great grandfather, both royal princes trained for the military and served in the Household Cavalry's Blues and Royals regiment, with William also experiencing the navy and air force.

After he graduated from the University of St Andrews, Prince William entered the Royal Military Academy Sandhurst in Berkshire in January 2006. Prince Harry had already been at the Academy since May 2005, having gone there straight from Eton. The princes had recently acquired a Private Secretary, Jamie Lowther-Pinkerton – known by the boys as JLP – who had first joined the Royal Household as Equerry to the Queen Mother while serving in the Special Air Service, attached to the Irish Guards. He had participated in the first Gulf War and during the conflict in the Balkans.

Lowther-Pinkerton's job as Private Secretary was to council and guide the princes to help them achieve their goals and reach their full potential. He was well placed to empathise with the young royals as he had also been to Eton and Sandhurst, and he knew that fulfilling their ambitions at that stage would give them the confidence and knowledge of the world to take on the royal duties to follow. As one of the Household said: "William does it flying out to the middle of the Atlantic in a Force 9, rescuing people. Harry does it on the front line in Afghanistan, and they can then look at anyone at the end of it and say 'Yes fine, I'm on these tramlines now and I know what I've got to do and it's not necessarily everything that I want to do but I know my duty. But, I also knew the day when I was a brave young thing."

Above all, Lowther-Pinkerton commanded the young princes' respect. As Harry said in his autobiography: "... JLP was a force, the product of Britain's finest military training, which meant, among other things, that he didn't deal in b******t. he didn't give it, didn't take it, and everyone, far and wide, seemed to know."

Military Training

Sandhurst is the establishment where all officers in any branch of the British Army receive their initial training. Regular Officer instruction

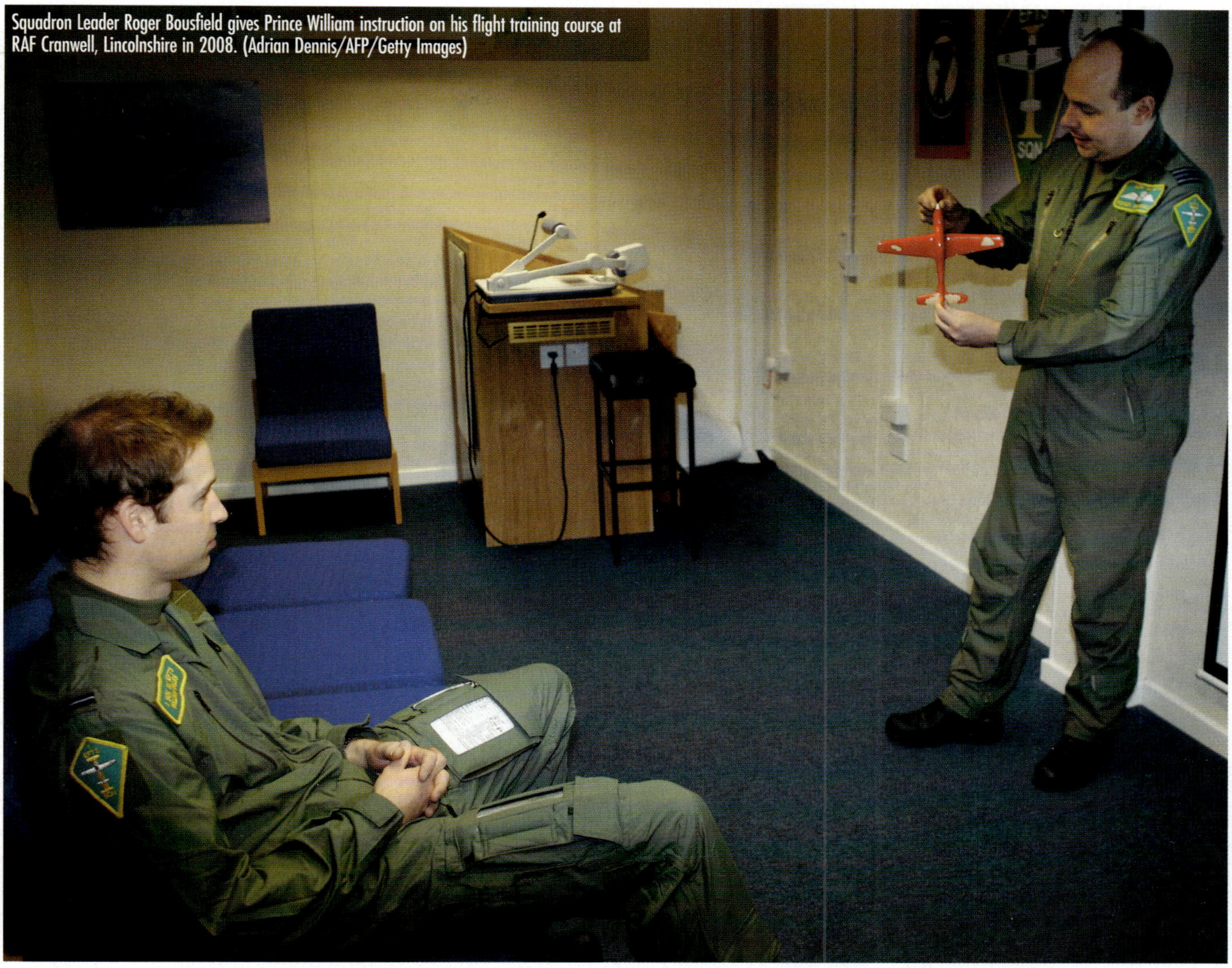

Squadron Leader Roger Bousfield gives Prince William instruction on his flight training course at RAF Cranwell, Lincolnshire in 2008. (Adrian Dennis/AFP/Getty Images)

at this world-renowned institution takes the form of a 44-week course broken into three terms, each of which concentrates on a different aspect of becoming a troop leader. First, the princes as Officer Cadets focussed on basic military skills, improving fitness and learning to make decisions. In that term the recruits learn survival and first aid skills, fieldcraft and how to use a rifle.

Then in the second term they learn leadership skills, with an emphasis on paperwork, and choose the regiment they want to join, which for both princes was the Blues and Royals section of the Household Cavalry. This is the second-most senior regiment in the British Army, only subordinate to the Life Guards by virtue of age. The Life Guards was formed during the reign of Charles II to be his bodyguards while he was living in exile after the English Civil War. The Blues and Royals was formed in 1969 by the merger of the Royal Horse Guards and the Royal Dragoons. Within the British Army, the Household Cavalry, that also contains five regiments of foot soldiers, focuses on providing reconnaissance experts, snipers, anti-tank specialists and intelligence gatherers. It combines these roles with ceremonial duties and members of the Household Cavalry Mounted Regiments – the Life Guards and the Blues and Royals – provide an escort to the monarch on major state occasions and a guard at the gates of Buckingham Palace.

The final term at Sandhurst is spent amalgamating the skills learned in the previous two terms on home and overseas training exercises. The exercises abroad involve working with other nations' armed forces as well as exchanges with Westpoint Academy in the US, America's premier officer training facility. After the 44 weeks, if Cadets have acquitted themselves well, they receive their commission as British Army officers.

Time at Sandhurst is a life-shaping experience. For the royals it meant the first time they were truly mixing with people outside their previously limited circles. Cadets qualify for Sandhurst on merit and can come from all walks of life and stages of education, and from anywhere in the ➲

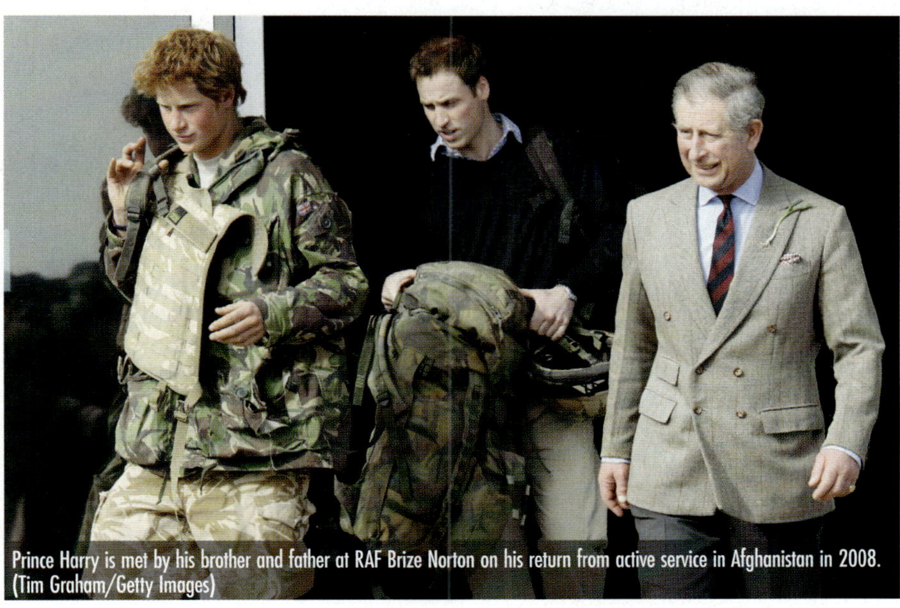

Prince Harry is met by his brother and father at RAF Brize Norton on his return from active service in Afghanistan in 2008. (Tim Graham/Getty Images)

Prince William and his squadron leader put theory into practice on the tarmac at RAF Cranwell in 2008. (Adrian Dennis/AFP/Getty Images)

Prince William in the cockpit of a Grob 115E light aircraft, known at the Tutor, while training at RAF Cranwell in 2008. (Adrian Dennis/AFP/Getty Images)

world. As William later said in a speech in front of the latest graduation group: "The friendships forged [at Sandhurst] will last a lifetime and you will have been fortunate enough to have shared experiences with people from many different backgrounds, countries, cultures and religions."

Prince William's Army Career

William graduated from Sandhurst in December 2006 as a Second Lieutenant in the Household Cavalry in charge of a troop of four Scimitar armoured reconnaissance vehicles. In the following year he made it to Lieutenant. However, despite The Queen giving approval for him to serve in frontline situations there was too much nervousness in government and higher military circles about the advisability of this, given his position at the time as third in line to the throne. So unlike his younger brother,

HMS Iron Duke, sailing in the Atlantic and intercepting drug-smuggling operations. On board he was crew on a Lynx helicopter. He then transferred his commission to the RAF and was soon promoted to Flight Lieutenant, learning the ropes as a search and rescue helicopter pilot. In 2010 he joined a Search and Rescue Training Unit in Anglesey, Wales to learn more advanced helicopter flying – carrying loads under the aircraft, flying low, at night and in mountainous terrain, and maritime rescue winching. At RAF Culdrose in Cornwall he was introduced to the large Sea King Mk3 navy helicopters used for rescues and then spent time back at RAF Valley observing genuine rescues and practising simulated ones. After completing 70 hours of live flying and 50 in a simulator he graduated as a fully trained search and rescue pilot. The officer who commanded Prince William's squadron, Wing Commander Mark Dunlop, said: "Flight Lieutenant Wales demonstrated the required standards needed for the award of Operation Captaincy. Due to the nature of search-and-rescue operations, the required standards are always set at a very high level. Operational captaincy carries the overarching responsibility for the safety of the aircraft, its crew and any casualties."

Over the next three years William took part in 156 rescue operations, including a tour of duty in the Falkland Islands as part of the British ⮑

William's time in the Blues and Royals was short-lived and he moved on to attachments with both the Royal Navy and the Royal Air Force (RAF), training as a Sub-lieutenant in the former and a Flying Officer in the latter, which equalled his army rank of Lieutenant.

Unlike his brother, who as the traditional second son of any aristocracy, was expected to follow a military career – either that or the church, but Harry chose the armed forces – Prince William's role was more of a profile-raising, diplomatic exercise. As a spokesperson from Clarence House put it: "As with the prince's previous attachments and visits, one of the aims is to highlight the important and often difficult work carried out by the men and women of the Armed Forces."

A spell at the Britannia Naval College followed, and service for a while on a Type 23 frigate,

Prince William and his girlfriend Kate Middleton arrive at the Central Flying School at RAF Cranwell, ahead of the graduation ceremony to present his RAF wings. (Tim Graham/Getty Images)

In flying with the RAF, Prince William was following in the footsteps of his father, Prince Charles, who completed his flying training 37 years earlier. (Adrian Dennis/AFP/Getty Images)

military contingent providing security to the islands after the Falklands Conflict of the 1980s. It was while he was in the Falklands that he became a Pilot in Command, taking full responsibility for his aircraft's operation and safety.

He ended active service with the RAF towards the end of 2013 and spent some time working on his charity projects before he went into retraining to become an Air Ambulance pilot.

Prince Harry's Army Career

Prince Harry was commissioned in April 2006 and joined his Blues and Royals regiment the following month as a Cornet, or Second Lieutenant. He then began a Troop Leaders' Course to qualify him to lead an armoured reconnaissance unit of 11 soldiers and four Scimitar vehicles, specialising in the gathering of battlefield intelligence. By December 2007, at the age of 23, Harry had been deployed to serve with the British Army in Helmand Province, Afghanistan. By April 2008 he had achieved two years with the regiment and was promoted to Lieutenant.

As someone in the direct line to the British throne, Harry's role in the military was not without controversy. There were sections of government that were of the opinion that it would be too dangerous for him to go into active service. However, the then Defence Secretary John Reid advocated on the prince's behalf, saying that he should be permitted to join a frontline troop. Iraq was mooted to be the first deployment for the newly qualified prince but, in the event, his high profile and the risk of kidnap in that country was deemed to potentially put not only himself but also his fellow soldiers at additional risk, so that move was not progressed. British Intelligence had learned that photographs of the prince had been circulated to its snipers with instructions that he was a prime target.

At the end of this rollercoaster of excitement and disappointment, and after additional training in the Yorkshire Dales, Canada and the US, Harry made it to the Afghan war zone, albeit in secret at first. He was put to work in Forward Air Control, coordinating the movements of combat, ground cover and medivac aircraft in the war zone. It was not the frontline position Harry craved but it tapped into his life experiences thus far and he was happy. "This was important work, patriotic work," he has said. "I was using skills honed in the Dales and at Sandringham, and all the way back to boyhood. Even to Balmoral. There was a bright line connecting my stalking with Sandy [the estate gamekeeper] and my work here now. I was a British soldier, on a battlefield, at last, a role for which I'd been preparing all my life."

Unfortunately, when the world press got wind of his presence in Afghanistan he was withdrawn on safety grounds. Another knock-back for the young prince but one that opened up a further opportunity when he spent the next 18 months training as an Army pilot before being chosen to learn to fly Apache attack helicopters. This led to his second experience of combat in Afghanistan. Newly promoted to Captain, he was deployed to Camp Bastion in September 2012 as a co-pilot and gunner attached to 3 Regiment, Army Air Corps where his superiors treated him very much as just one of the team. Like everyone else he lived in a shared room in accommodation made from shipping containers and he joined the thousands of other British military personnel eating in the canteen and using the gym. The Major General in command at the time said, "The only thing special we did for him was we had a place identified as a safe house in case the base came under attack."

In July 2013 he qualified as an Apache Aircraft Commander after a tough six-hour flying assessment around the UK, planning and delivering patrol orders, flying and navigating through controlled air space and performing a simulated low-level air attack while simultaneously dealing with mock aircraft emergencies and other diversions to his attention. The regiment's commanding officer, Lieutenant Colonel Tom de la Rue, said it was "a tremendous achievement for Captain Wales who passed with 'flying colours'". His new status put him at the very top of his Army profession.

Following his successful active career, Prince Harry took up a role as Staff Officer at HQ London District, the main headquarters for all British Army units within the perimeter of the M25 motorway. He was put in charge of a variety of London projects and Army events and particularly worked as part of the Personal Recovery Unit, helping to formulate recovery plans for wounded, injured and sick Army personnel and arranging necessary support for them to lead productive lives.

In early 2015 Harry left the armed forces after 10 years but continued to work in the Personal Recovery Unit as a volunteer. ●

Prince Harry makes the 45-second scramble from the 'very high readiness' tent to his Apache helicopter at the British-controlled Camp Bastion in Afghanistan in 2012. (John Stillwell/Getty Images)

Captain Harry Wales takes to the cockpit of his Apache attack helicopter towards the end of his tour in Afghanistan in 2013. (John Stillwell/Getty Images)

Wearing the uniforms of their respective services, William and Harry lay wreaths at the Cenotaph on Whitehall in central London on Remembrance Day 2015. (Carl Court/Getty Images)

Prince Harry, in his capacity as Captain General Royal Marines, carries out a Green Beret presentation at Dartmoor National Park in Devon in 2019. (Finnbarr Webster/Getty Images)

CIVVY STREET

Their time in the armed forces at an end, the princes took on other forms of work alongside their royal duties, building on the skills they had acquired.

Prince William checks over his helicopter as part of his work as a pilot with the East Anglian Air Ambulance in 2015. (Stefan Rousseau/WPA/Getty Images)

On his final shift as an Air Ambulance pilot in 2017, Prince William discusses the day with one of the crew at Cambridge Airport. (Heathcliffe O'Malley/WPA/Getty Images)

For Prince William, the logical next step from flying with the RAF Search and Rescue team based at RAF Valley in Anglesey, Wales, was to join the Air Ambulance Service. This vital emergency transport charity is funded entirely by donations and the proceeds of its own weekly lottery draw and the prince operated as part of a team of specialist doctors and critical care paramedics. He served with the East Anglian Air Ambulance (EAAA) for two-and-a-half years, from early 2015 to mid-2017, donating his salary back to the charity.

William flew from a base at Cambridge Airport which was the optimum place for the air ambulance's catchment area of Cambridgeshire, Norfolk, Suffolk and Bedfordshire. At the time, William and Catherine were living at Anmer Hall in Norfolk, an hour and 20-minute drive from the airport but still more convenient for getting to work than a central London address. The EAAA pilots were all employed by a private company, Bond Air Services, which was later taken over by Babcock, an international defence company that also supplies equipment and personnel to emergency services. Flying the EAAA helicopter on day and night shifts was his main job, although the service arranged his rotas around his royal duties supporting The Queen at events. A spokesman for Kensington Palace said: "The duke sees this as a true form of public service, helping people in their most difficult times."

Prince William, Camilla and Prince Charles show their support for Prince Harry's Invictus Games at the opening ceremony in London in 2014. (Chris Jackson/Getty Images)

The two princes share a joke on William's iPhone during the 2014 Invictus Games at the Lee Valley Athletics Centre on the outskirts of London. (Max Mumby/Indigo/Getty Images)

Although it was a role and responsibility he thoroughly enjoyed, the work did take a mental toll. After one particularly traumatic case of a child who had been hit by a car, he found it difficult to process his emotions. "It was like someone had put a key in a lock and opened it without me giving permission to do that," he said in an interview shortly after. "I felt like the whole world was dying. It's an extraordinary feeling. You just feel everyone's in pain, everyone's suffering."

He went on: "I was lucky enough that I had someone to talk to at work in the Air Ambulance because mental health where I was working was very important. Talking about those jobs definitely helped, sharing them with the team, and ultimately meeting the family and the patient involved who made a recovery, albeit not a full recovery, but made a recovery."

Stressful experiences such as this, and an incident where a young man attempted suicide, focussed the prince's mind on mental health issues in general and he has made this one of the priorities of his charity work. In a BBC documentary he said of the EAAA: "There are some very sad, dark moments, and we talk about it a lot. But it's hard. You try not to take it away with you, but it can be quite difficult."

In July 2017, the prince left the air ambulance service to concentrate on his charity work and official duties, which were increasing. In a statement he wrote: "It has been a huge privilege to fly with the East Anglian Air Ambulance. Following on from my time in the military, I have had experiences in this job I will carry with me for the rest of my life, and that will add a valuable perspective to my royal work for decades to come."

Harry's Army Legacy

In 2013, Prince Harry represented the Crown on a tour of the Caribbean and America. While he was in Colorado he was invited to an event called the Warrior Games, a sporting event for wounded soldiers of the American Army. "Most were natural athletes," he recalled, "and they told me these games had given them a rare chance to rediscover and express their physical talents, despite their wounds. As a result it made their wounds, both physical and mental, disappear. Maybe only for a moment, or a day, but that was enough. Once you've made a wound disappear for any length of time, it's no longer in control – you are."

These encounters inspired Harry to formulate an ambition to hold a paralympic event for wounded armed forces personnel from all over the world using the facilities at London's Olympic Park. Just before he finished his ten-year army career, he began to put serious work into making his dream of the games become a reality.

In November 2013, with the help of his new Private Secretary Ed Lane Fox, nicknamed Elf by the prince, he approached Sir Keith Mills, mastermind behind the 2012 London Olympics. Initially reluctant to come out of semi-retirement, Sir Keith agreed and the very demanding timetable began. Harry wanted the start of the games to coincide with the 100th anniversary of the start of World War One, which was the following September.

The name of the event was to be the Invictus Games, named after the 1875 poem *Invictus* written by William Ernest Henley that had been suggested to the prince and his team by one of the Royal Marines. The Invictus Games Foundation was subsequently formed to support wounded, injured and sick service men and women and veterans around the world. On the Foundation website Prince Harry is quoted: "These Games have shone a spotlight on the 'unconquerable' character of servicemen and women, their families and the 'invictus' spirit. These Games have been about seeing guys sprinting for the finish line and then turning round to clap the last man in. They have been about teammates choosing to cross the line together, not wanting to come second, but not wanting the other guys to either. These Games have shown the very best of the human spirit."

In the first Games, 300 competitors represented 13 countries that had been involved with the UK in recent military campaigns. For the 2023 Games, postponed since 2021 because of the Covid-19 pandemic, 22 countries have confirmed they will be sending athletes.

Aside from his work on the Invictus Games and fund-raising for it, Prince Harry stepped back from being involved in royal duties at the beginning of 2020. Since then the prince has been working with charities in the United States and has a continuing involvement with the Sentebale project in Lesotho. He and Meghan set up the Archewell Foundation, a not-for-profit organisation liaising with businesses for charitable purposes. ●

To highlight the second Invictus Games in Orlando, Florida the following year, 2015, Prince Harry watches wheelchair basketball at a US Warrior Games with the then First Lady Michelle Obama. (Saul Loeb/AFP/Getty Images)

Invictus

By William Ernest Henley

Out of the night that covers me,
    Black as the pit from pole to pole,
I thank whatever gods may be
    For my unconquerable soul.

In the fell clutch of circumstance
    I have not winced nor cried aloud.
Under the bludgeonings of chance
    My head is bloody, but unbowed.

Beyond this place of wrath and tears
    Looms but the Horror of the shade,
And yet the menace of the years
    Finds and shall find me unafraid.

It matters not how strait the gate,
    How charged with punishments the scroll,
I am the master of my fate,
    I am the captain of my soul.

Prince William performs his ceremonial duty at a Trooping the Colour parade in 2017 as the Colonel of the Irish Guards regiment of the Household Cavalry. (Arthur C James/dreamstime.com)

As a result of their experiences of their mother's death and in the army and air ambulance, the princes are keen to support mental health campaigns and in 2016 attend a party for volunteers at The Mix youth service. (Danny Martindale/Getty Images)

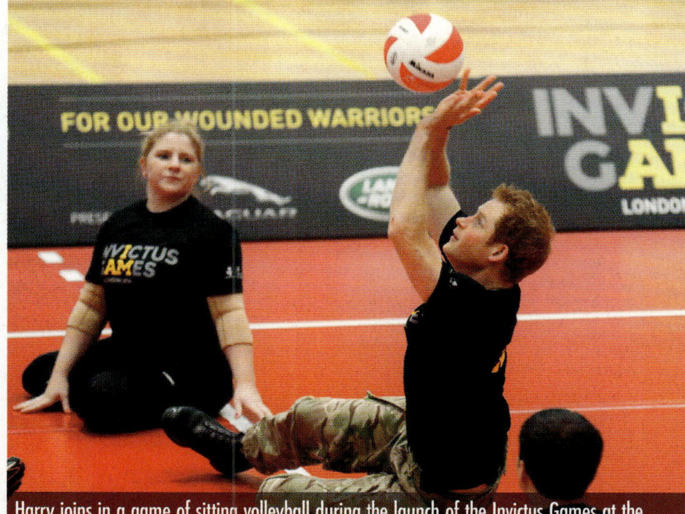

Harry joins in a game of sitting volleyball during the launch of the Invictus Games at the Queen Elizabeth Olympic Park in 2014. (Max Mumby/Getty Images)

Helping to inspire young people to get active, volunteer and work for issues close to their hearts, Prince Harry takes to the stage for We Day UK in 2019. (Jo Hale/Redferns)

A WEALTH OF
CHARITY WORK

Traditionally, members of the royal family have been patrons for a wide variety of charities. Their choice of causes has often been influenced by their experiences.

The royal family has been involved in charity work since the 18th century when George II became a patron of the Society of Antiquaries. According to the royal family's official website: "The benefits of Royal patronages are twofold. They add status to an organisation, and visits and involvement from a Royal Patron can often bring much-needed publicity."

This has certainly been the aim of the two princes in their choice of charities to support. Although they have lent their names to some high-profile organisations, they have also shone a light on areas that have had less of an impact on the public consciousness, following the example of their mother, Princess Diana.

Apart from supporting already established charities as their Patrons, there are a number of charitable organisations that were set up by the royals themselves in areas to which they felt a particular affiliation. Princes William and Harry's great grandfather, George VI, when he

Princes William and Harry help volunteers packing emergency relief boxes at a Red Cross depot in the city of Bristol for victims of the 2004 tsunami in the Indian Ocean. (Tim Graham/Getty Images)

development between the ages of 14 and 24, first for boys and then the following year for girls also. Participants now take part in each of four sections of the scheme: Volunteering, Physical, Skills and Expedition.

When he was Prince of Wales, King Charles greatly increased the number of charities founded personally by a royal. The umbrella title of The Prince's Charities encompasses 19 organisations, 18 of which were the initiative of the prince himself, including The Prince's Trust. He started the Trust with his severance pay from the Navy in 1976 to help young people from 11 to 30 struggling with education or unemployment. He also founded initiatives such as The British Asian Trust, In Kind Direct, Business in the Community and The Prince's Countryside Fund. They all reflect the interest areas of the King – harmonious communities, protection of the countryside, regeneration and recycling, among others.

The princes' mother, Princess Diana, added her influence to her sons' later choices by the way she espoused causes that, at the time, were avoided by the mainstream. She highlighted, for example, the misery caused by HIV and Aids when the disease first hit epidemic proportions and the world was terrified by the rapid spread and high death toll. She raised the profile of problems many countries were having in dealing with the aftermath of war and unexploded landmines. And she tackled the stigma surrounding rough sleepers on the streets of Britain's capital city that was hampering funding for solutions. By her support, she elevated the needs of many overlooked charities and made supporting them acceptable in influential circles.

William's Charities

Like their father and grandfather, Princes William and Harry have embraced causes in areas that are closest to their hearts and experiences. When they were young children, Princess Diana made a point of taking them to see life outside the palace walls – how some of the less fortunate and disadvantaged in our society managed. She took them to hospitals and to shelters for rough sleepers, which

was Duke of York, founded the National Playing Fields Association in 1925. Being very keen on sport himself, and an accomplished tennis player, he wanted to protect parks and open spaces in urban areas used by people for sporting activities, exercise and fresh air that might otherwise disappear to development.

Prince Philip's desire was to open up chances for young people, regardless of their background, culture or ability, to experience anything they might want to try in life. To that end he set up the Duke of Edinburgh Award scheme in 1956 to support young people's

William, Harry and singer/songwriter Joss Stone rehearse in the rain for the 2007 Concert for Diana to raise money for her charities. (Max Mumby/Indigo/Getty Images)

Prince Harry with his young friend, six-year-old Mutsu Potsane, in 2006. The prince had first met Mutsu on his gap year two years previously and was inspired by him to form the Sentebale charity. (John Stillwell/Getty Images)

sparked William's interest in helping those whose circumstances in life had led them to lose their homes and take to the streets. Centrepoint, the homeless charity, became his first patronage in 2005 when he was in his early 20s and he promoted the cause by spending a night sleeping out in London and taking a turn as a *Big Issue* seller, the publication that provides an income for the homeless.

The Chief Executive of Centrepoint, Seyi Obakin OBE, recalled the occasion that came about following a dinner Prince William hosted for donors to the charity who had spent a Sleep Out night in Leadenhall Market in London to raise money. Obakin had light-heartedly questioned whether the prince would himself have taken part in the Sleep Out, given the opportunity. William, he said, would have, but he didn't want a soft option, he wanted to properly experience what it was to have nowhere but the streets to sleep. "I decided to do it with him," he said, "having instigated this thing. Four of us set out at midnight – myself, Prince William, Jamie [the prince's Private Secretary] and one police protection officer… We looked around, found a little place where there might be a bit of shelter, in our case a set of wheelie bins, put down our cardboard, covered ourselves as best we could and hunkered down for the night."

After a "bone-chilling" night, when the temperature reached -4 and they were almost run over by a road sweeping van, the four walked

On a trip to Africa in 2010 the princes visited a number of projects supported by their charities. Here they put gloves on a young boy at an education centre in Lesotho. (Chris Jackson/Getty Images)

through London for about 45 minutes to get to a shelter where they could take turns to shower. "None of the people we passed blinked," said Obakin. "You wouldn't expect Prince William to be walking down the road at that time in the morning in a beany hat, tattered jeans, looking dishevelled like a rough sleeper." Although

people later questioned the wisdom of the exercise from a security point of view, Obakin did not see there was a problem. "Actually," he said, "the anonymity was security itself. No one expected him to be there."

Reflecting his interest in wildlife and the environment, William is also a patron

Prince Harry and Prince Seeiso of Lesotho on stage at a Coldplay concert in London in 2016 to raise money for the Sentebale charity the two princes set up. (Max Mumby/Indigo/Getty Images)

A visit to the London Eye wheel in 2016 to celebrate World Mental Health Day with the princes' charity Heads Together, part of the Royal Foundation. (Samir Hussein/Getty Images)

their mother, might have given them much-needed support.

Heads Together has undertaken a number of initiatives, including partnering with the Football Association in 2019 to create a campaign – spearheaded by Prince William – using football to change attitudes about mental health, helping to encourage more men to feel comfortable talking about their mental health and able to support their friends and families through difficult times. In 2021 the prince unveiled the Blue Light Together Initiative, a package of mental health support for emergency workers, recognising the unique stresses they face as part of their daily work.

On the death of The Queen and the accession of Prince Charles to the throne, Prince William was elevated to Prince of Wales. Coincident to this, Prince Harry decided to step away from being a working royal and so the foundation they formed now goes by the title Royal Foundation of the Prince and Princess of Wales. It could be seen as a culmination of the boys' upbringing by another Princess of Wales who wanted to instil a sense of responsibility in them to care for those less fortunate. In an interview she gave to the BBC, Diana said: "I want them to have an understanding of people's emotions, people's insecurities, people's distress, and people's hopes and dreams."

Harry's Charities

Prince Harry, with his military background, has embraced a number of charities that support veterans and deal with other after-effects of conflict around the world. Among these is the HALO Trust, which was a cause that was very close to Princess Diana's heart. It is a joint UK/US NGO that specialises in the removal of hazardous debris left behind by war, particularly land mines.

Harry also lends his support to Help for Heroes, Joining Forces that helps service members with post-military careers, The Warrior Programme and Walking with the Wounded. He also espouses charities connected to disadvantaged young people around the world, some of them inspired by his partnership with Meghan Markle, such as Free the Children and

of charities such as Tusk Trust that works to protect endangered species, the Prince's Rainforest Project, African Wildlife Foundation and WildAid. In 2020 William founded the Earthshot Prize, an annual award that gives recognition to the work of organisations and countries all over the world that have pioneered extraordinary solutions to some of the globe's most pressing environmental issues.

As parents, William and Catherine also espouse a number of child-related causes such as Children in Crisis, BeatBullying, Unicef, WellChild and Teenage Cancer Trust. As he has said: "You get affected by things that happen around the world a lot more as a father, just because you realise how precious life is."

The brothers and their partners created The Royal Foundation that, like The Prince's Charities, acts as an umbrella for a number of different initiatives allied to William and Harry's main interests, everything from mental health to early childhood, wildlife conservation to climate change. It's stated aim is that it "...mobilises leaders, businesses and people so that together we can address society's greatest challenges."

One of the campaigns it embraces is Heads Together, a coalition of eight mental health charity partners aiming to change the national conversation on mental health. It focuses on raising awareness that, just as we have to look after our physical health, we also have to take

care of our mental wellbeing. Its covers areas where good mental health has possibly been underestimated – the workplace, school and in the armed forces. It is a group of organisations that, had they existed at the time the princes lost

Sporting heads Together headbands, William, Catherine and Harry put their heads together to change the national conversation around mental health. (Nicky J Sims/Getty Images)

The Heads Together mental health charity again benefitted from the princes' support when they took part in its training day for the London Marathon in 2017, along with William's wife Catherine. (Alastair Grant/WPA Pool/Getty Images)

On the day of the 2017 London Marathon the two princes and Kate were at the start to see the runners setting off and cheer them on. (Max Mumby/Indigo/Getty Images)

the PeyBack Foundation that gives grants to improve the lives of abused and neglected young people in some US states.

Harry's first solo involvement with charity began during his gap year between school and military training in 2004, when he spent time in the southern African country of Lesotho. There he met and formed a friendship with Prince Seeiso, with whom he spent two months, living in the country and learning about how the Aids epidemic has ravaged the lives of the population since the late 1980s, particularly its children. His visit culminated in the creation of the charity Sentebale in 2006. This organisation, the name of which means Forget-me-not in the Northern Sotho language, looks after orphaned young people and those who do not otherwise have access to decent schooling.

Seeiso is also a second son to a king and this must have resonated with a prince who was already conscious of his role as the British royal family 'spare' to the heir. Harry was fresh from a slightly tarnished teenage, with the tabloid press publishing stories of underage drinking and drug taking, so the trip gave him the opportunity to escape the scrutiny and throw himself into something he came to feel passionate about. In Prince Seeiso, despite their 20-year difference

in ages, he found someone who understood something of what he was experiencing.

As Seeiso said in an interview about the man he nicknamed H: "Before I met him I had total sympathy for him because I am a second son as well. And being number two has an effect on you and the way people perceive you. I knew how it felt to be judged against someone who is squeaky clean, quiet, reserved and perfect. My brother, like H's brother William, ticked all the right boxes, and I ticked all the wrong boxes. Fortunately, we do not have an aggressive media in Lesotho because I am sure if we had there would have been stories about me rather like the ones printed about H."

The Lesotho prince and Harry formed a friendship that has lasted to this day and he and his wife, Princess Mabereng, were the only foreign royals to be invited to Harry and Meghan's wedding. The other lasting friendship formed in Lesotho was between Harry and an orphan called Mutsu Potsane, who he first met in 2004 when he was four years old. Now grown up, Mutsu helps to run Sentebale and was also a guest at the prince's wedding, one of 10 representatives of Sentebale invited to Windsor Castle.

The woman who helped to organise the prince's first visit to Lesotho, Malineo Motsephe, summed up his contribution to their society when she said: "Here he is known as Mohale, which means brave man or warrior. He dared to come here and live with us and his concern and empathy for the disadvantaged children of our country has made a difference and will continue to make a difference."

Now that he has moved to the United States and is no longer involved in royal duties, Prince Harry has set up his own charity foundation with his wife Meghan as Duke and Duchess of Sussex. Called Archewell, it is named after the couple's son Archie and its core purpose it states is: "to do good. Our three main pillars of focus are to build a better world online, to restore trust in information, and above all, to uplift communities." The charity also includes filmmaking and audio branches partnered with Netflix and Spotify that aim to use the power of storytelling to highlight "shared humanity and truth through a compassionate lens".

The ethos of the prince's new charity shows the direct influence all his experiences in life to date have had on his outlook. ●

William and Catherine took on another role later in the race - as water dispensers at one of the refuelling stations along the route. (Chris Jackson/WPA Pool/Getty Images)

The 2018 Royal Foundation Forum to showcase the Foundation's programmes uniting businesses in partnership with mental health, environment, children's and wildlife charities. (Chris Jackson/WPA Pool/Getty Images)

Little legs dangling, two small boys sit beside their father amidst the finery and gold braid for the pageant of the Beating Retreat ceremony on Horse Guards Parade in London in 1989. (Tim Graham/Getty Images)

IN THE NAME OF THE
MONARCH

As senior members of the royal family, both princes were expected to be present at and take part in official assignments from an early age. Some of these duties were a pleasure, some sad, and some undoubtedly tedious.

It was on William's very first royal trip abroad, to Australia when he was less than one year old, that he was given the affectionate sobriquet Wombat by his mother, which stuck with him throughout his childhood. It was a nickname inspired by the circumstances of being in the animal's native country, William would later say, not because he looked like one! Playing a role on an official tour, albeit a limited one as he did not appear in public too many times on the trip, was unusual in one so young. But Princess Diana did not want to leave her young child at home alone for more than a month and so, accompanied by nannies, he was taken along and proved to be a great hit with his parents' hosts.

It was the same with domestic events. In their Sunday best outfits, hair neatly groomed and manners polished, the youngest of princes was expected to turn out as ambassadors at many official events. They had to stand or sit still and behave themselves as they were presented to foreign dignitaries, politicians and businesspeople, and treated to traditional ceremonies and pageantry not necessarily filled with excitement and interest for a small child. Like young Prince Louis at the King's coronation in Westminster Abbey, they might occasionally have been put into the care of a nanny for a short break if the event was a long drawn-out one, but they were not expected to make a fuss, fidget or make a noise, no matter how bored they were.

Meet and Greet

When they were older the functions and the people perhaps got more interesting, their royal status getting them behind the scenes and to places to which ordinary people have

Prince Charles, Prince William and Prince Harry listen to speeches at the opening of a fountain in Hyde Park, London, in 2004, built in memory of Princess Diana. (Getty Images)

William and Catherine are ferried round the KLCC Park in the city of Kuala Lumpur during their Diamond Jubilee tour of the Far East in 2012. (Gwoeii/Shutterstock)

no access. But their primary role at every event was not personal enjoyment but be ambassadors and patrons, highlight their charities, the UK and its businesses. Part of their remit has also always been to make themselves available to the public so people can see them, have the chance to take selfies, shake hands, give flowers, chat to them for a moment and maybe even give them a hug.

The first mass encounter of ordinary people by a monarch happened in Canada in 1939 when The Queen's father, George VI, and the Queen Mother mingled with a crowd of veteran soldiers, boy scouts and members of the public at the unveiling of Ottawa's World War One war memorial. It was a hitherto unknown experience that the Queen Mother never forgot. "I lost my heart to Canada and to Canadians, and my feelings have not changed with the passage of time," she later said.

Routine royal walkabouts began with The Queen in 1970 when she and Prince Philip were on a tour of Australia and New Zealand.

She felt there was a chance to meet more of her people, rather than just a few officials and local dignitaries, if she left her car and went for a stroll. It went down so well it became a regular event, even though it strained the royal protection team no end, worrying about their principals' safety.

Royal tours are no holiday, packed as they are with meetings and greetings, attending concerts and dinners, displays of local customs, tours of museums, galleries and local businesses, unveilings and openings. On top of that there are often long distances to be travelled in short time spans, but making the effort to get out of the car was something The Queen encouraged all the senior royals to do. If any of her family or entourage were to suggest she might get too tired, The Queen always claimed you were only tired if you were bored by people and since she never was, she did not feel weary.

William on Tour

From his first overseas royal engagements with his parents in Australia and New Zealand at only nine months of age, William went on to travel a modest amount but with many years between. Then, in 2005, when he left university, he represented The Queen for the first time alone at two events in New Zealand commemorating the end of World War Two. While he was there, he also indulged his passion for rugby and supported the British and Irish Lions.

In 2010 his position as President of the Football Association took him to many of its opening ceremonies and to countries bidding to host the World Cup. And the same year he was in New Zealand again for the opening of the new Supreme Court building. He then went on to Australia to, among other engagements, tour areas around Melbourne that had been subjected to devastating bush fires. He returned to both countries in March 2011 after the Christchurch earthquake and Queensland and Victoria floods.

After his marriage to Catherine in the April the couple undertook a nine-day tour of Canada and then went on to the US for a further three days. While there, William played in ➲

William and Catherine dancing with the islanders of Tuvalu in the South Pacific on their tour of the Far East in 2012. (Samir Hussein/WireImage)

The princes witness Stage 1 of the British leg of the Tour de France cycle race in Harrogate, Yorkshire in 2014. It was the first time the historic race had started in a country other than France. (Chris Jackson/WPA Pool/Getty Images)

Prince Harry greets crowds in The Mall on his way to The Patron's Lunch in 2016, a street party on her 90th birthday to celebrate The Queen's patronage of more than 600 charities. (Oliver Simon/dreamstime.com)

a polo match at the Santa Barbara Polo and Racquets Club, unaware that it would become his brother's club when he moved his family to California nearly a decade later.

In 2012, as part of The Queen's Diamond Jubilee celebrations, the royal couple travelled to the Far East, visiting Singapore, Malaysia, the Solomon Islands and Tuvalu. That was the last official foreign excursion until 2014 when the Australian and New Zealand governments invited the couple to visit with their son George.

There was a tour of Canada towards the end of 2016 when Princess Charlotte went along with her brother. And in 2022 there was a week-long, whistlestop tour for the couple to Belize, Jamaica and the Bahamas. Their support of the Earthshot Prize for innovative environmental work took them to Boston, Massachusetts at the end of 2022.

In between there were trips, alone and together, to the US, Japan, China, a few African nations, India, Poland, Germany, Israel and Palestine, several Scandinavian countries and Pakistan, to name just a few. All in all, Prince William has made official visits to around 47 countries in his life with the tally of events

An informal meeting with US President Barack Obama and his wife Michelle at Kensington Palace in 2016, during their London visit a few months before the end of his presidency. (Stephen Crowley/AFP via Getty Images)

Touring Pinewood Studios in west London in 2016 and meeting the creative team working on the latest *Star Wars* movie is an ideal opportunity for a light sabre duel between brothers. (Adrian Dennis/Getty Images)

William and Catherine with Prince George and Princess Charlotte arrive at Victoria Airport in British Columbia, Canada, on their royal tour in 2016. (Salma Bashir Motiwala/Shutterstock)

The powerful royal triumvirate of William, Catherine and Harry, hosting a tea party in the grounds of Buckingham Palace in 2017 for the children of military personnel who have died serving their country. (WPA Pool/Getty Images)

Prince William goes walkabout in Esplanade Park in Helsinki in 2017 on the 100th anniversary of Finnish independence. (Aleksandra Suzi/Shutterstock)

Prince Harry and his wife Meghan in Melbourne, Australia, on their 2018 official tour to the country where they were representing The Queen. (Robyn Charnley/dreamstime.com)

Prince Harry lays a wreath in Liwonde National Park in Malawi in 2019 in memory of Mathew Talbot of the Coldstream Guards who was killed on an anti-poaching raid. (Dominic Lipinski/PA Wire)

included in those visits well in excess of 300, without including walkabouts and official dinners.

Harry on Tour

Royal duties abroad began for Prince Harry soon after he left the army, although he had also done his share of goodwill trips with his parents and in his gap year from school. However, in 2012 he represented The Queen on his own, on a nine-day tour of Belize, the Bahamas and Jamaica as part of Her Majesty's Diamond Jubilee celebrations, and then on to Brazil on behalf of the Foreign and Commonwealth Office to strengthen ties between the two countries.

This tour was the first of many for the prince alone, often linked to armed forces events, such as a World War One service in Belgium or a Remembrance Service in Afghanistan, but also for diplomatic reasons such as his visit to South Africa to present the Order of the Companions of Honour to Archbishop Desmond Tutu and see the work of the Nelson Mandela Foundation. This was followed by trips to Nepal, Canada and the US, where he first saw the Warrior Games for wounded veterans that inspired the international Invictus Games he founded.

Then in 2016 he went to several Caribbean countries – Antigua & Barbuda, St Kitts and Nevis, St Lucia, St Vincent and the Grenadines, Grenada and Barbados, as well as visiting Guyana, again on behalf of the Foreign Office. He was present at celebrations of the 50th anniversary of the island of Barbados gaining its independence and he reviewed the Barbadian military, police and medical personnel – a role that must have been strange for him as until then he had been the one on the receiving end of a royal army review.

In 2018 and now a married man, Harry toured Australia, Fiji, Tonga and New Zealand with Meghan. The following year they went to Morocco to view projects focussed on women's empowerment and female education. Their last big tour before stepping back from royal service was to South Africa with their son Archie when they met with Desmond Tutu. Harry then went on to Malawi, Angola and Botswana, visiting wildlife conservation projects and the minefield where Princess Diana had walked with the HALO Trust, all causes he is passionate about. ●

The Duke and Duchess of Sussex meeting crowds in the city of Birmingham where they were marking International Women's Day in 2018. (mattkeeble.com/Shutterstock)

GIRLFRIENDS AND WIVES

One of the greatest influences in anyone's life is the person they choose to be their partner. For the royal princes those choices have had a special significance as they have chosen a work partner as well as a wife.

They say one in 10 students at St Andrews meets their future spouses there. In fact, when the university principal made a speech at Prince William's graduation, he alluded to the time-proven statistic and cautioned the alumni of 2005 that they may already have met their life partners. At the time, that was by no means a sure thing with William and Catherine Middleton. They had been studying together for four years and living in the same halls of residence, St Salvator's, which is known by the students as Sallies, then in a shared four-bedroomed Edwardian house off campus and finally a shared cottage outside the town.

Kate obviously knew who William was when they first met in the Sallies corridor where their rooms were, and she was slightly intimidated. In an interview together when they were married she recalled: "I went bright red when I met you and sort of scuttled off, feeling very shy about meeting you... it did take a bit of time for us to get to know each other, but we did become very close friends from quite early on."

Their romance grew gradually from a basis of friendship and mutual support in their first year of academia. "At St Andrews we were friends for over a year first and it just sort of blossomed from then on," William has said. "We just spent more time with each other, had a good giggle, had lots of fun and realised we shared the same interests and just had a really good time."

They were both sporty and enjoyed spectating as well as taking part. They skied, played tennis, surfed, dived and swam and they loved watching rugby. Kate had no affectations, she was just a normal girl from a middle-class background who didn't stand out in a crowd, she didn't wear much make-up and wasn't a flirt, although she was bright and funny and popular with boys. Her father and mother had worked for an airline as ground and flight crew respectively until they set up their own business selling children's party packs. So Kate grew up in a household where hard work was expected and there were no airs and graces even when the family fortunes improved.

Initially at St Andrews Kate went out with a fourth-year student and she and William were simply good friends and housemates, but by their second year they were dating. When they moved out of the halls of residence and into their first shared house with two others, though, they were still just friends. On his 21st birthday, Prince William allowed reporters a glimpse of ➲

Prince Harry and his long-term girlfriend Chelsy Davy sharing a love of polo at an international match at the Guards Polo Club in Windsor Great Park in Berkshire in 2006. (Max Mumby/Getty Images)

Harry and Chelsy Davy leave a Service of Remembrance at Holy Trinity Church in Windsor, Berkshire in 2008. (Ben Stansall/Getty Images)

shopping ("I enjoy shopping, actually," he said. "I get very carried away.") and had learnt some cooking while at Eton, producing a gourmet meal wasn't so easy. As he explained in an interview: "When I was trying to impress Kate I was trying to cook these amazing fancy dinners and what would happen was I would burn something, something would overspill, something would catch on fire and she would be sitting in the background just trying to help, and then basically taking control of the whole situation..." Kate chipped in: "I would have to wander in and save something that was going wrong."

When he joined St Andrews, William asked his friends to call him Steve if they were talking about him, to avoid anyone picking up on what could be exploited as royal gossip. Even so, "princely gossip was constant around the town", said one of his contemporaries, recalling the slightly less-than-normal life of a prince at university. "Spotting him was never hard. He was tall, and usually followed by a column of girls with dreams of becoming the next queen of England. They had learned his schedule by heart and shared the prince's location via text messages. He also had two bodyguards around at all times, who tried to be discreet but were easy to recognise after a while."

By the time they graduated in 2005, William had gained a 2:1 honours degree in Geography and Kate the same grade in Art History, and they were 'an item' as the press were quick to publicise.

Harry and Chelsy

At about the same time William and Kate were coping with press photographers on the ski slopes, Harry was embarking on a relationship with Zimbabwean jewellery designer Chelsy Davy. Harry was in his gap year when they met, having just finished his A-levels at Eton. He was, by that time, a first-class polo player and the pair spent time together at the Berkshire polo club. Then Harry went off to Australia to spend part of his year of experiences working on a cattle station while Chelsy went to South Africa to study economics at the University of Cape Town.

A few months later Harry was in southern Africa, about to spend a couple of months on the next stage of his gap year working on a building

the thought processes of an eventual royal heir to the throne – an insight into considerations that most other young men embarking on a romance don't have to worry about. "If I fancy a girl and I really like her and she fancies me back, which is rare, I ask her out," he said. "But at the same time, I don't want to put them in an awkward situation because a lot of people don't quite understand what comes with knowing me."

Their romance took off slowly as level-headed Kate demonstrated that she could cope with what came with knowing William. While he was in the St Andrews environment the press largely abided by their agreement with the Palace that they would leave the prince to enjoy his university career in as normal a fashion as possible. The same didn't hold good outside of the university, though. In 2004, William and Kate went skiing together to the royals' favourite resort of Klosters in Switzerland. The tabloid press was all over the trip, trumpeting headlines of the couple's new-found relationship. It was a breach of the agreement by the *Sun* newspaper that led to harsh words from the Palace. For their part, newspaper editors complained that they had been assured they would have regular official access at key moments for both princes and, in fact, they had had little opportunity when it came to William's 21st. The bun fight was a lesson for Kate in what to expect from having an alliance with a royal prince but she was not fazed by the attention. In the end, Sir Michael Peat, Prince Charles Private Secretary, agreed the press could have access to William

once a term for the rest of his time at St Andrews.

Keeping Life Normal

Out of halls of residence and having to cater for himself the prince found that, although he could cope with a shared rota for cleaning and

The newly married Duke and Duchess of Cambridge wave to the crowds as they travel down the Mall from Westminster Abbey to Buckingham Palace in the 1902 State Landau in 2011. (Max Mumby/Indigo/Getty Images)

A blissfully happy Prince Harry and his newly announced fiancée Meghan Markle pose for official photographs in November 2017. (Chris Jackson/Getty Images)

project in Lesotho. It was a return to the continent where he'd spent recuperation time after his mother died. A favourite part of the world that took him away from all the furore in Britain. He contacted Chelsy and invited her to a barbecue at the residence of the British Consul General and their relationship developed from there and lasted almost continuously for the next seven years.

In his autobiography Harry described why he felt so immediately attracted to her. "She seemed immune to that common affliction sometimes called *throne syndrome*. It was similar to the effect that actors and musicians have on people, except with actors and musicians the root cause is talent. I had no talent – so I'd been told, again and again – and thus all reactions to me had nothing to do with me. They were down to my family, my title, and consequently they always embarrassed me, because they were unearned… Instead we talked about the main thing we had in common – Africa."

In 2011, the couple parted ways. The romance had run its course, but they remained friends. To an extent, relentless press interest every time they had a cooling off period and time apart to pursue their own interests, had prevented them from being just another couple with their ups and downs. In an interview, Chelsy said the attention of the press was horrible because, "it was so full-on; crazy and scary and uncomfortable. I found it very difficult when it was bad. I couldn't cope."

Shortly after, Harry had a short-lived affair with TV presenter Caroline Flack but it ended very quickly after the press picked up the story. Then a year after the split from Chelsy, Prince Harry was introduced to actress and model Cressida Bonas by his cousin, Princess Eugenie. That relationship lasted for two years, until 2014 when they had an amicable parting. Cressida had also found it difficult to handle the newspaper reporters and photographers cataloguing the couple's every move in public.

It seemed as if there would never be a woman for Harry who could cope with the inevitable barrage of interest from the intrusive press machine.

The Three of Us

When William and Kate became seriously involved and it was obvious that it was a relationship that would potentially last into marriage, Harry was drawn into their orbit. Up to then, it had been the two boys united in their traumatic experiences and facing the world with each other's support. As Harry said about an interview he gave when he was in Africa, "I told the reporter that no one but Willy understood what it was like to live in this surreal fishbowl, in which normal events were treated as abnormal, and the abnormal was routinely normalised."

Prince Harry and Meghan Markle departing from the press call in the sunken gardens at Kensington Palace where they announced their engagement. (Steve Back/Getty Images)

Now the dynamic was set to change and as the outsider to the budding relationship it was Harry who stood to lose the most. However, he took an instant shine to his soon-to-be sister-in-law. "I liked seeing Kate laugh," he said in his autobiography. "Better yet, I liked making her laugh. And I was quite good at it. My transparently silly side connected with her heavily disguised silly side. Whenever I worried that Kate was going to be the one to take Willy from me, I consoled myself with thoughts of all our future laughing fits together, and I told myself how great everything would be when I had a serious girlfriend who could laugh along with us."

The three royals shared a love of many things, especially sports, and common goals in doing good work for the charities they supported. Young, healthy and full of life they formed a powerful triumvirate at official and unofficial events.

A Royal Wedding

In her *Panorama* television interview in 1995, Princes Diana mourned the lack of love in her life. She spoke about telling William about her separation from his father and how she told him: "… if you find someone you love in life you must hang on to it and look after it, and if you were lucky enough to find someone who loved you then one must protect it."

William took this to heart when he met Catherine and although they did part for a short time after university, they eventually decided to marry. They had been discussing it for about a year before William proposed on holiday in Kenya with some of their friends. The timing made it a surprise for Kate but William had taken the ring with him – his mother's sapphire and diamond engagement ring. "I had been carrying it around with me in my rucksack for about three weeks before that," he said in an interview, "and I literally would not let it go. Everywhere I went I was keeping hold of it because I knew this thing, if it disappeared, I would be in a lot of trouble."

The couple would have liked a small private wedding at the country church near Kate's parents' home in Berkshire, but that was never going to happen. So instead William said he wanted "…a day that is as enjoyable as possible, for as many people as possible". When drawing up a proposed guest list the Lord Chamberlain took this pronouncement a little too far for the prince, who looked askance at the number of people on it who were unknown to him, invited simply for protocol's sake. Concerned, he turned to his grandmother The Queen, the story of which he

told to royal biographer Robert Hardman: "I rang her up the next day and said: 'Do we need to be doing this?' And she said: 'No. Start with your friends first and then go from there.' She made the point that there are certain times when you have to strike the right balance. And it's advice like that, which is really key, when you know that she's seen and done it before." After that, William saw or spoke to The Queen on the phone every week, even if it was just for half an hour, and she helped him, on a practical as well as an emotional level, to plan and execute the big day.

Despite being a pared down, more personal event, the marriage was still a royal wedding. It was held at Westminster Abbey on April 29, 2011, conducted by the Dean of Westminster and solemnised by the Archbishop of Canterbury with around 2,000 people in attendance. Prince William wore the red dress uniform as Colonel of the Irish Guards and a full peal of the Abbey bells was rung for three hours at the end of the service. The couple travelled to Buckingham Palace in the 1902 State Landau and posed on the famous Buckingham Palace balcony to wave to the crowds before the wedding breakfast.

Catherine's entry into the royal family gave William a staunch supporter to help him with all his royal duties but also be a companion and confidante, giving him an escape from the restrictions and ceremony into a normal family life. This, she said in an interview, was what inspired both of them about the prince's grandmother. "All the time William and I are so struck by The Queen's sense of duty and commitment. And I think to do that by yourself would be a very lonely place to be. But I think to have the support of your husband there by your side on those occasions – and behind closed doors as well – I think is really special."

Meghan Joins the Family

Five years after his brother's wedding Prince Harry met his future bride, Hollywood actress Meghan Markle. His first sight of her was on a friend's Instagram feed and he asked to be put in touch. Meghan was in London to watch tennis and meet up with friends, including Princess Eugenie, who she knew through their mutual friend, fashion designer Misha Nonoo.

Harry and Meghan began communicating by text and finding they had a shared love of Africa. Dinners at a secluded table in a London restaurant followed and then a safari in Botswana that was the definitive start to the couple's romance. Meghan was filming

the TV series *Suits* in Canada and had already been commuting to London on a regular basis, when the fancy took her, but now it became something she had to do. It was too difficult for Harry to fly to Canada without attracting the attention of journalists wanting to know the reason for the trip. They had decided to keep their relationship secret, partly until they were sure of each other and partly to protect both of them from unwelcome stalking by the paparazzi.

In late 2016, the commitment they had made to each other meant the next step was meeting the family. The arrangement was to introduce Meghan first to Princess Eugenie's mother, the Duchess of York, but The Queen had chosen the same day to visit. In the event, the meeting with his grandmother passed off without a hitch

Hiding the nerves, Harry shares a friendly joke with William as they await the arrival of his bride Meghan at St George's Chapel, Windsor in 2018. (Owen Humphreys/AFP/Getty Images)

Prince Harry and his bride Meghan Markle descending the steps from the West Door of St George's Chapel in Windsor in 2018, having just become a couple. (Ben Stansall/AFP/Getty Images)

The newly married Harry and Meghan are driven through the streets of Windsor in the Ascot Landau escorted by the Household Cavalry Mounted Regiment. (Hadrian/Shutterstock)

after Meghan had been given a quick lesson in how to curtsy and address The Queen. "It was all very pleasant," Harry recalled, "Granny even asked Meg what she thought of Donald Trump. (This was just before the November 2016 election, so everyone in the world seemed to be thinking and talking about the Republican candidate.) Meg thought politics a no-win game, so she changed the subject to Canada."

William was the next in line for an introduction. Harry recalled the moment the couple popped over to Kensington Palace. "After a wait the door opened and there was my big brother, a bit dressed up. Nice trousers, nice shirt, open collar. I introduced Meg, who leaned in and gave him a hug, which completely freaked him out. He recoiled. Willy didn't hug many strangers. Whereas Meg hugged most strangers. The moment was a classic collision of cultures, like flashlight-torch, which felt to me both funny and charming."

A month later the relationship came to the notice of the press and the pursuit of a good story began both in the UK and at Meghan's home in Canada and her mother's in Los Angeles. Many column inches were filled with details that varied from factual laced with spin to out-and-out manufactured gossip. Despite Harry's anger, the advice from the Palace publicity machine, and from his family, was to just ignore it.

The adverse publicity died down and then attitudes changed when Harry and Meghan's engagement was announced. A tour of the four countries of the UK brought out crowds of well-wishers. As Harry said: "A total departure from the tone and tenor of the tabloids, and also a reminder: the British press wasn't reality."

The date and venue for the wedding were chosen – St George's Chapel, Windsor, on May 19, 2018. As a second son, Harry had less of the pomp and circumstance to worry about for his wedding. There was no onus on the invitations conforming to protocol and having to include foreign dignitaries and titled nobility. Harry wore the frock coat uniform of the Blues and Royals regiment of the Household Guard and the congregation consisted of the couple's friends and family.

The Dean of Windsor conducted the ceremony and, as with William and Catherine, the Archbishop of Canterbury married them. Meghan later revealed that that was the second time the Archbishop had married them. "Three days before our wedding, we got married – no one knows that – but we called the Archbishop and said, 'This thing, this spectacle is for the world, but we want our union between us.' So the vows that we have framed in our room are just the two of us in our backyard with the Archbishop of Canterbury." ●

Prince Harry embraces the sports his wife grew up with as the couple pose with the New York Yankees baseball team ahead of a game against the Boston Red Sox in London in 2019. (Peter Nicholls/Getty Images)

Facing a television film crew and press photographers at the age of two, Prince William is encouraged by his father Prince Charles at a press call in the gardens of Kensington Palace in 1984. (Keystone/Getty Images)

THE HATED
PRESS

The greatest influence on the opinions and behaviour of the two princes has been the world's media. Ever-present in their lives since birth, it has been a monster machine that has dogged their footsteps and changed their lives.

It speaks volumes that William has said that his first experience of not being the literal focus of attention from the media was when he stayed on the Lewa game reserve in Kenya in 2001 at the age of 19. During his stay, the Craig family, who owned Lewa, organised the capture of a large bull elephant that had outgrown the area of the Conservancy. It was to be transferred to another, larger game park.

William helped with the operation but, unusually, his royal presence was not remarked at all – all the publicity and photographer attention was on the elephant and its journey. Quite a refreshing change for someone who had spent his whole life to date looking into the front end of dozens of camera lenses on every occasion he took part in.

The upside of being a desirable property in the eyes of a media keen to retain readers and viewers is that your presence as a royal prince at a charity event gets that charity's work propelled into the public consciousness. This increases support and donations and reaches the attention

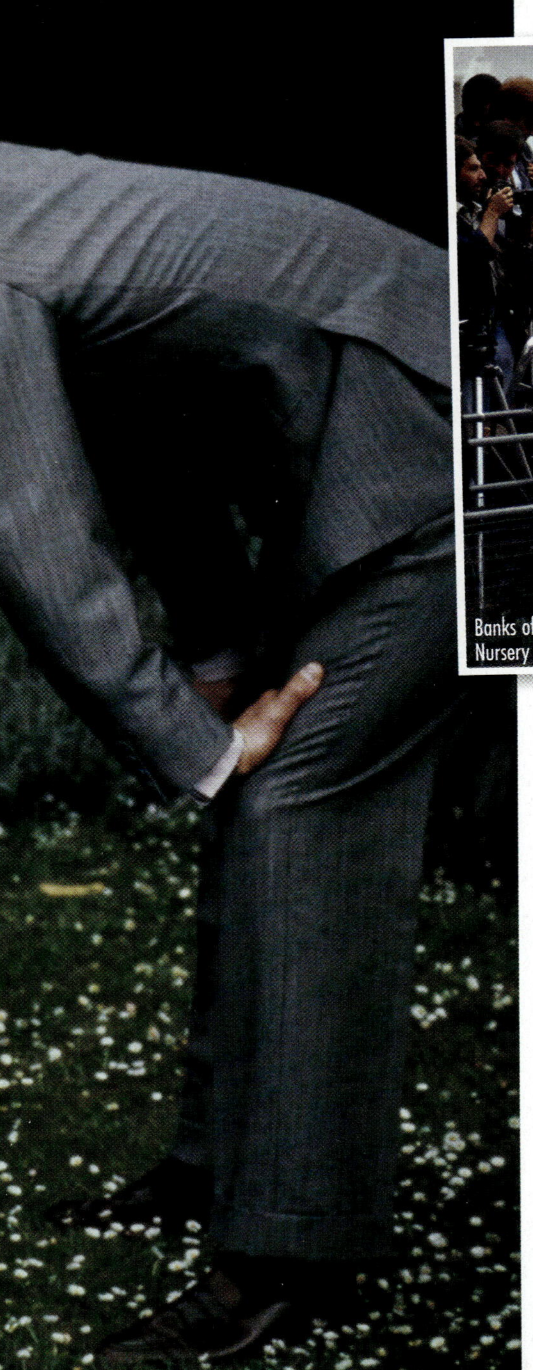

Banks of press photographers wait patiently to photograph a three-year-old Prince William arriving for his first day at Jane Mynor's Nursery School in 1985. (Tim Graham/Getty Images)

of potential recipients of the charity's help who may not have come across its work before. These are possibly the only cases for a royal when an intrusive camera lens can be a welcome thing. For the rest of the time it is something to be tolerated, understanding that with the royal role comes a duty to be visible to the people whose taxes pay for the monarchy.

The royal family has been treading a fine line ever since photography became the norm for recording world events. They have become used to negotiating their privacy. Offering up defined times and places, managing access to photographers in return for being left alone. They have also routinely arranged their own official images to distribute at key moments in their lives – such as Catherine issuing regular updates on the progress of her children by snapping them herself on their birthdays.

The Royal Arrangements

These moves with the media are designed to give the newspapers access to the senior royals on a regular basis and satisfy their quest for interesting stories for their readers

in a controlled way. They were stepped up from the 1960s, when newspapers became less rigidly news focussed and embraced celebrity gossip. Photocalls were seen as a way of making it less necessary for editors to buy images from the paparazzi. Making that trade less lucrative is the ardent wish of celebrities around the world. Putting up with photocalls with official photographers, hours of arranged interviews with writers and authorised recordings of conversation with the public on official walkabouts is one thing. Jostling crowds of pushy freelancers shouting personal questions, being constantly chased by paparazzi photographers and discovering their hidden long lenses have captured intimate moments, those are a completely different matter.

Prince Charles, through long experience of dealing with every sort of situation, has developed a sanguine attitude to the rogue press that Harry, for one, has found hard to deal with. In his autobiography he relates how he had sought advice from his father when the press got hold of some gossip about Harry allegedly cheating at exams at Eton. "He said what he always said. 'Darling boy, just don't read it.' He never read it. He read everything from Shakespeare to White Papers on climate change, but never the news." Not that Charles was unaffected all the time as Harry went on to say: "He did watch the BBC, but he'd often end up throwing the controller at the TV."

The Palace mantra has always been "never complain, never explain" and on most occasions this has been what has held sway until the storm has passed over. It was a philosophy that Harry has found hard to accept, aggrieved that senior royals are never allowed to defend themselves publicly. The lawsuits over privacy intrusion and phone hacking that he and Meghan have launched have been a cause of much friction between the couple and the Palace and, by inference, the rest of the family.

Nevertheless, at times of extreme media pressure, the royal family has often found ways to get their story across without seeming to be on the defensive. Prince Charles' television interview with Jonathan Dimbleby during the break-up of his marriage was unprecedented at the time, but an example of how a modern royal was going to counter with dignity what his estranged wife and others were saying about

him. The Palace's 'good publicity' machine now cranks up at opportune moments to provide distractions to many of the negative reports, another source of annoyance for Prince Harry when he has believed that 'planted' stories have not been in his interest.

The Official Royal Photocall

From being very small boys, William and Harry have had to get used to presenting themselves to hordes of photographers at organised photo shoots. So William's first experience of staring into the lens of a camera came on his first day at nursery school when the world wanted to see that big step in his young life. In the lead-up to the day, Charles and Diana had written to every newspaper editor requesting that after the photocall the three-year-old be left to come and go to school unobserved. They agreed they would next make him available for photos when he performed in his school nativity play. A friend of Diana's who was there that day said: "There was this bank of photographers, all on ladders. And everyone was shouting, 'William, William, William!' It must have been terrifically difficult for a child that age to understand."

Holidays were other occasions where an organised shoot on the first day ensured peace to enjoy the rest of the holiday without intrusion. This has been particularly so on skiing holidays through the years where the first hours on the slopes are taken up with posing in happy family groups for a line of photographers. These have become quite casual affairs with the royals joking with newspaper staff and freelancers who they have got to know over the years.

Of course, there is nothing like a royal engagement, wedding or birth to bring the press – authorised and unauthorised – out in force. Familiarity with some of the accredited old hands has aroused some sympathy with William for people who are only doing their jobs and who have consideration for what is appropriate behaviour. When he and Catherine faced the cameras on their return from Kenya and his marriage proposal, William singled out two long-standing photographers who had been taking his picture since he was born. Always polite, they had requested the couple look specifically at their lenses, which they duly did, and gave them excellent shots for their papers. ➲

Prince William engages with the hordes of journalists and press photographers who have greeted him on his visit to an education centre in Glasgow, Scotland, in 2001. (Tim Graham/Getty Images)

Members of the press camped outside the entrance to Kate Middleton's parents' home in Bucklebury in Berkshire, hoping to catch a glimpse of her in 2010. (Photocritical/dreamstime.com)

The Curse of the Paparazzi

Paparazzi photographers, by contrast, are despised by both princes. These independent snappers specialise in taking pictures of the rich and famous, particularly in intimate or compromising situations, in order to sell them for a lot of money to the more sensational sections of the mass media. William and Harry take difference stances when it comes to attempting to control the paps.

For Prince William the way forward is to seek the backing of British law. He analyses legal rulings on invasion of privacy and how far it can be claimed that something is 'in the public interest', as evidence that regulations have to be tightened officially to make a difference. The ultimate aim would be to have a ban imposed on the publication in the press of any images that haven't been sanctioned by the subjects, as is the case in France. However, this hasn't stopped the paparazzi in France from taking illicit images

anyway, and selling them abroad, but it is a start on upholding a person's right to privacy.

For Harry it is more of a head-on challenge to the 'public interest' label and taking it through the courts. His language in his autobiography, when addressing the type of photographers he very much blames for his mother's death and for making his wife's life intolerable, is frank and four-lettered.

When Prince Harry began his relationship with Meghan Markle the sensationalist press went into overdrive, captivated by the novelty of a royal having a partner who was American, an actress, a divorcée and of mixed race. The more that the most unscrupulous journalists dug into her background, the more they found that could be elaborated and speculated on, and used to provide gossip-style copy for their readers. An ulterior motive or a desire to defy royal conventions was ascribed to many of the things she did, and a rivalry with her future sister-in-law

was seen as a delicious supposition to fill column inches. According to Harry, because there was a reluctance by the Palace to comment on any of the allegations and an inability of other members of his family to speak out for fear of damaging their tenuous relationship with the press, there developed an information void that was filled by yet more salacious stories.

The first recourse to the courts was the step taken by Meghan when a British newspaper published a private letter she sent to her estranged father just before her wedding. It was a risky move because it threatened to give rise to even more adverse publicity about the couple. Prince Harry, however, backed her measure in a statement on the effects of the press in general on his wife. "Though this action may not be the safe one, it is the right one. Because my deepest fear is history repeating itself. I've seen what happens when someone I love is commoditised to the point that they are no longer treated

As part of the Palace's agreement to grant the press access at specific times in the princes' lives, Harry gives a television interview while serving in Afghanistan in 2012. (John Stillwell/Getty Images)

In 2018, ranks of paparazzi wait outside Pop Brixton, a community space where Reprezent Radio is hosting an event about combatting knife crime in London, hoping to snap royal guests Prince Harry and Meghan Markle when they emerge. (Lorna Jane/dreamstime.com)

or seen as a real person. I lost my mother and now I watch my wife falling victim to the same powerful forces."

No Let-up

Despite Harry and Meghan's attempts to fight back, the paparazzi was again in full cry when they rented a country home in the Cotswolds. Helicopters buzzed the property while photographs were taken through their windows. The plan to have a country retreat in Britain had to be abandoned.

In November 2019 the couple borrowed a house on Vancouver Island in Canada. It was a temporary escape from the seemingly endless press intrusion as Harry described: "After a few days we needed supplies. We ventured out timidly, drove down into the nearest village, walked along the pavement like people in a horror movie. Where will the attack come from? Which direction? But it didn't happen. People didn't freak. They didn't stare… Everyone knew, or sensed, that we were going through something. They gave us space, while also managing to make us feel welcome, with a kind smile, a wave. They made us feel like part of a community. They made us feel normal."

Unfortunately, the idyll couldn't last after one of the British papers gave away their address. On their return to the UK, they made the momentous decision to step back from being royals. "Part of this job is putting on a brave face," said Harry in a television interview, "but, for me and my wife, there is a lot of stuff that hurts, especially when the majority of it is untrue."

Prince Harry's next counter to the British press was a television interview with presenter Oprah Winfrey. For the couple it was a chance to set the record straight in a way they had been dissuaded from doing in the UK. It was not viewed in such a positive light by their friends

The couple appear after the event at Pop Brixton and are immediately lit up by dozens of flash bulbs as they cross the street to their waiting car, heads down. (Lorna Jane/dreamstime.com)

and family and further damaged relations between the brothers.

Then came the publication of Harry's memoir, *Spare*, and the subsequent publicity interviews that laid bare the prince's opinions about not only the press but the support he felt was lacking from his family. The stage was set for a permanent estrangement from the royal family caused mainly, it seemed, by a rogue British press and, perhaps understandably, by a cautious press office.

Journalist and royal expert Tina Brown gave her opinion to UK trade publication *Press Gazette*, of Prince Harry suing News Group Newspapers, Mirror Group Newspapers and the Mail titles in 2023 for criminal information gathering. As she researched a chapter of her book about the surveillance of the royal

family she said: "I was shocked… I really hadn't quite understood the torment that the young adolescent Harry was put through with the hacking. As well as being tormented by the media scrutiny, he was in a constant state of like, 'how do they know? Who's betraying me? Which of my friends can I trust?' It created such a level of insecurity for him about who he could trust, a real paranoia because the papers would seem to know about things before they'd hardly even been scheduled…

"When you think about that, you do understand why Harry thinks 'you know what, I have the funds now, I don't care, I've got nothing to lose. I'm not one of the royal family really anymore. I don't have to care about the ongoing collusion between the press and the royal family so I'm just gonna go for it.'" ●

THE NEXT
GENERATION

Becoming parents inevitably changes perspectives on life but for William and Harry there's an added dimension of wondering what their children will experience in a modern monarchy.

Prince George was born third in line to the throne on July 22, 2013. Like his father before him he arrived at St Mary's Hospital in west London in its private healthcare Lindo Wing. In scenes reminiscent of Prince Charles and Princess Diana introducing their sons to the world on the steps of the hospital, William, Catherine and George faced banks of photographers and film cameras before getting into the family car and driving home to Kensington Palace.

The godparents for the new young prince included some of the people who have exerted a positive influence on Prince William's life – his university friend Oliver Baker, Julia Samuel, who was a close companion of Princess Diana, his cousin Zara Tindall and Jamie Lowther-Pinkerton who had been his Private Secretary and has remained a trusted support in the background ever since.

From the outset Prince William was determined to be as ordinary a modern dad as his status allows. In an interview with American broadcaster CNN shortly after George's birth he related how he had been sharing getting up in the night to care for his baby and, like any new father, how he was missing his sleep. In that respect, his job as an RAF Search and Rescue pilot helped as he had to spend time away from home. "Well, as a few fathers might know," he said, "I'm actually quite looking forward to going back to work to get some sleep. So I'm just hoping the first few shifts I go back I don't have any night jobs."

Before he was a year old, Prince George had gone on his first royal tour. Like his father George made the three-week trip to Australia and New Zealand with his parents and thanks to his presence the good-will visit was even more successful. As royal correspondent Nicholas Witchell wrote at the time: "From the moment he was carried down the aircraft steps by his mother on their arrival in New Zealand on Monday 7 April, Prince George was the star of the show. He has only appeared twice (other than at airports) and even then the settings have been carefully managed – first at a specially convened playgroup in Government House, Wellington and then, memorably, at a new enclosure at Taronga Zoo in Sydney [where he was introduce to an Australian native animal, a bilby that had been given the name George].

"On each occasion the appeal of a nine-month-old future king has upstaged even the glamour of a future queen consort and her husband."

In May 2015, the couple's second child Princess Charlotte was born. Thanks to the Succession to the Crown Act in 2013, which rewrote history to make all children in the direct family line equal, regardless of their sex, the little girl became fourth in line to the throne. This inevitably moved Prince Harry's position down the line and led to questions from the press that he felt offensive. As he said: "I was an uncle again, and very happy about it. But, predictably, during one interview that day or the next a journalist questioned me about it as though I'd received a terminal diagnosis. I thought: first of all, it's a good thing to be further from the centre of the volcano. Second, what kind of monster would think of himself and his place in the line of succession at such a time, rather than welcoming a new life into the world?"

Charlotte joined her brother in becoming an early globe trotter, accompanying the family on a royal tour of Canada in 2016 and to Germany and Poland in 2017. And all of the royal couple's children have been present at high-profile occasions such as Trooping the Colour ceremonies, the memorial service for Prince Philip, The Queen's state funeral and the King's Coronation.

Public appearances notwithstanding, from the word go William and Catherine have wanted their children to be brought up as normally as being part of the royal family will allow. In a television appearance in 2016 William said: "I would like George and Charlotte to grow up being a little bit more simple in their approach and their outlook, and just looking after those around them and treating others as they would like to be treated themselves."

The children are helped in that respect by Kate's background, coming from a working middle-class family. It gives them the opportunity for the children to spend time at their maternal grandparents' home, away from palace staff and protocol, just free to play with cousins and friends. Like most couples they have to consider how to give an equal share of ➲

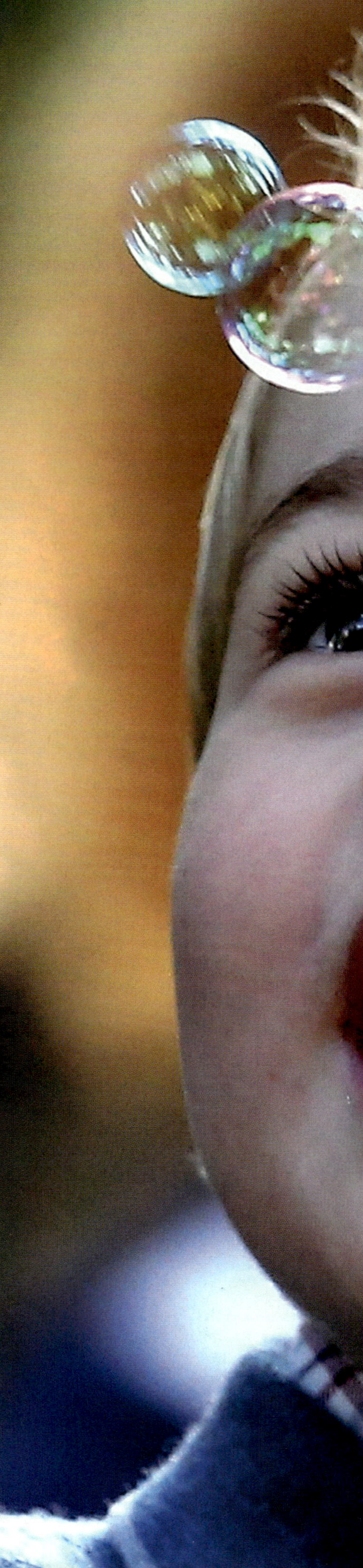

Like any three-year-old child, Prince George is enthralled by bubbles blown at a children's party for military families during a royal visit to Canada in 2016. (Chris Jackson/Getty Images)

their children's time to respective grandparents, particularly at Christmas.

When The Queen was alive, all the members of her immediate family were expected to spend the holiday season at Sandringham, taking the famous walk to church on Christmas morning. However, in 2016 The Queen gave approval for her grandson and his wife to take their children to their Middleton grandparents in Bucklebury in Berkshire instead. This followed a similar break with tradition that had been granted in 2012, the year after they married and when Catherine was pregnant. She had been suffering badly from morning sickness and The Queen may have realised that time with her mother would be more beneficial to her than being in a large royal congregation.

In their early married life the royal couple kept household staff to a minimum. When William was serving with the RAF Search and Rescue in Anglesey they only employed a cleaning lady and on their move to their accommodation in Kensington Palace they took on no more than a housekeeper. As their royal duties have increased so have they had to take on more staff, assistants to arrange their work schedules, press officers and a nanny. Maria Borrallo, trained at the world-famous Norland College, has been looking after the children since 2014 when Prince George was

eight months old. The arrival of Prince Louis in April 2018 completed her group of royal charges.

The children have made significant differences in both William and Catherine's lives. "I'm a lot more emotional than I used to be," William said. "I never used to get too wound up or worried about things. But now the smallest little things, you well up a little more, you get affected by the sort of things that happen around the world or whatever a lot more, I think, as a father. Just because you realize how precious life is and it puts it all in perspective."

In 2023, William and Kate moved from Kensington Palace to the four-bedroomed Adelaide Cottage in Windsor Home Park, the private estate of 655 acres of land on the eastern side of Windsor Castle in Berkshire. The children's school, Lambrook, is nearby, so boarding isn't necessary. Unlike their father, the children's preparatory school years will be spent at home.

A Change in Approach

When the Duke and Duchess of Sussex became parents for the first time in May 2019 they bucked the royal trends. Harry and Meghan did not want their children to become immediate public property so the baby's place of birth, the private Portland Hospital in Westminster, London, was kept secret, only to be discovered

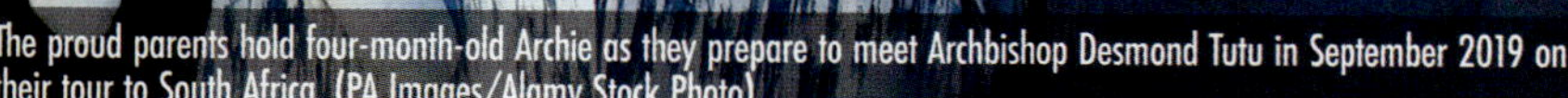
The proud parents hold four-month-old Archie as they prepare to meet Archbishop Desmond Tutu in September 2019 on their tour to South Africa. (PA Images/Alamy Stock Photo)

when his birth certificate was made public some weeks later. By the time Buckingham Palace announced the birth of Archie Harrison Mountbatten-Windsor his parents had already taken him home to Frogmore House in Windsor.

Naturally, therefore, there was no photocall on the steps of the hospital as Harry's parents and brother had agreed to. It was two days later that photographers were invited to Windsor Castle to take pictures to share with the world. His christening further broke with convention in that the names of his godparents were not revealed. Guarding his son from the world was, in a way, guarding his memories of his mother as Harry said in his memoirs, relating a trip to the south of France to stay with Elton John the family took when Archie was an infant. "Time and again I'd see an expression cross Archie's face and it would bring me up short. I nearly said so to Elton, how much I wished my mother could hold her grandson, how often it happened that, while hugging Archie, I felt her – or wanted to. Every hug tinged with nostalgia; every tuck-in touched with grief. Does anything bring you face-to-face with the past like parenthood?"

Prince William, Catherine and their children George, Charlotte and Louis, arriving at Lambrook School near Ascot in Berkshire in 2022 for a preview visit. (Jonathan Brady/Getty Images)

The couple's second child, Princess Lilibet, was kept even further out of the public eye. She was born on June 4, 2021 in the Santa Barbara Cottage Hospital in California, making her the first royal baby to have dual UK/US citizenship. This time there was no Palace announcement, but one from Harry and Meghan's Press Secretary and a statement on their Archewell website two days after her birth. Pictures of the little girl have all been taken by the couple themselves, with only one being officially released to the press, six months after her birth, and the rest posted on their social media pages. Again, the full list of her godparents has never been revealed, although one is rumoured to be filmmaker Tyler Perry, who lent his Los Angeles home to the couple when they first moved to the States.

The Queen only met her great granddaughter when she was a year old and her parents brought her with them when they returned to the UK to celebrate the Platinum Jubilee. After The Queen's death Harry and Meghan decided that their children would take the titles of Prince and Princess as they are entitled to by the letters patent issued by King George V in 1917. ●

Prince Harry holds a new-born Archie Mountbatten-Windsor while Meghan looks on after the baby's private christening in 2019. (Dominic Lipinski/Getty Images)

Prince Louis sits on his father's knee to watch The Queen's Platinum Jubilee pageant in The Mall in London in June 2022. (Max Mumby/Getty Images)

A PARTING OF THE WAYS

The changing attitude of the two brothers towards each other happened gradually but eventually profoundly affected both of their lives and their father's.

Throughout their years growing up and into adulthood Princes William and Harry were firm allies, understanding the position they were in and mutually supporting everything they did. Like brothers everywhere their relationship wasn't without its disagreements and conflicts, jealousies and rivalries but overall it was a loving one. A shared history of happiness and profound sadness, good times and a bad ones, had bonded them into a Willy and Harold team against a world of restricted movement and guarded speech.

As they grew older their lives took different paths and their differing characters began to assert themselves. As a very young child William had been the naughty one, the more forward one, while Harry was quiet and more reserved. When they entered teenage William became more studious and, while still enjoying himself, he tended to be quite conservative and disciplined. Harry had a more rebellious teenage, getting into scrapes that sometimes made it into the press. The difference between an eventual heir to the throne and his brother who had less of the pressure of obligation to duty began to show, in a similar way to The Queen and her younger sister Margaret. One of them knew they were born to bear the responsibility of monarchy while the other chafed at the restrictions and requirements to live up to expectations when they had no fundamental role to play, apart from being a support to their sibling.

The break-up of their parents' marriage and their mother's untimely death inevitably united the two princes closely for many years. When they met their partners and started families of their own, as often happens in the closest of siblings, they entered different worlds with new allegiances.

Like brothers the world over the princes have had disagreements and fights, even physical ones, over the years. One such occasion was remembered by Diana's confidante, alternative healer Simone Simmons, when it culminated in their mother saying to the boys: "You must promise me that you will always be each other's best friends. And never let anyone come between you."

Arguments in adulthood, though, tend to be much more damaging. While William began to grow further into his royal role,

Brothers who once had so much in common, now struggle with their differences. (Samir Hussein/WireImage)

Harry was moving into a position that took him away from the world he had known up to then. The attention from the paparazzi and a negative tabloid press had always preyed on the younger prince's mind since the death of his mother. But this intensified as he began to build relationships with women and culminated when he became engaged to Meghan Markle. The sensationalising of her background and

misrepresentation of a lot of what she did and said, made for upsetting headlines. Her interactions with the royal family were more often than not highlighted in a hostile light that could not be turned off.

The fact that the Palace publicity machine seemingly did nothing to defend her, aggrieved and infuriated the prince and set him against not only the institution but his family. He

Still maintaining cordial relations, William and Catherine, Meghan and Harry arrive for the Christmas Day service at St Mary Magdalene Church in Sandringham at the end of 2018. (Samir Hussein/WireImage)

challenged the Palace adage "never complain, never explain" and questioned the age-old custom of always attempting to keep the press 'on-side'. He could not, as his father had so often urged him, just not read what they were writing. When it came to making the woman he loved miserable and tormented, he felt he had to act, even though that put him in direct conflict with his father and brother.

A family rift opened up that led to Prince Harry stepping back from official duties and relinquishing most of his royal titles. The crisis came to a head at the beginning of 2020 when the couple returned to the UK, having made a temporary escape from the media spotlight in Canada. The end of their time abroad had come about because the press discovered their whereabouts. When asked in 2019 about coping with the pressure of media attention, Meghan had said: "In all honesty I have said for a long time to H – that is what I call him – it's not enough to just survive something, that's not the point of life. You have got to thrive." These latest experiences had brought into focus their inability to thrive under existing circumstances.

The prince made the decision that the only way they might have a chance of living in any form of peace would be if he and his family spent half the year outside the country, continuing to work for their charities but not on royal duties. His statement was posted on the couple's Instagram account without reference to the Palace, saying: "After many months of reflection and internal discussions, we have chosen to make a transition this year in starting to carve out a progressive new role within this institution. We intend to step back as 'senior' members of the Royal Family and work to become financially independent, while continuing to fully support Her Majesty The Queen."

The arrangement was later clarified in a statement from the Palace saying that the Duke and Duchess of Sussex had agreed to no longer represent The Queen formally or receive public funds for royal duties, effective from spring 2020. The statement from The Queen was warmer in tone: "Following many months of conversations and more recent discussions, I am pleased that together we have found a constructive and supportive way forward for my grandson and his family. Harry, Meghan and Archie will always be much loved members of my family. I recognise the challenges they ➲

William and Harry unveil a bronze statue of their mother, Princess Diana, in the sunken garden at Kensington Palace in 2021. The princes had jointly commissioned it from sculptor Ian Rank-Broadley. (PA Images/Alamy Stock Photo)

The rift that has caused the royal brothers to turn their backs on each other may in time heal. (Dominic Lipinski/AFP via Getty Images)

have experienced as a result of intense scrutiny over the last two years and support their wish for a more independent life.

"I want to thank them for all their dedicated work across this country, the Commonwealth and beyond, and am particularly proud of how Meghan has so quickly become one of the family. It is my whole family's hope that today's agreement allows them to start building a happy and peaceful new life."

Coming Together

In recent years, following the departure of Prince Harry and his family to the United States, only important events have brought the brothers back together. On each occasion they have demonstrated that they still have regard for each other and a shared history that will always connect them. The first event that saw the princes side by side was the royal ceremonial funeral of Prince Philip in April 2021, where they united to support their grandmother in her grief. Covid-19 restrictions were very much in force and only 30 guests attended the service. The two princes followed their grandfather's

Viewing the floral tributes to The Queen outside the gates of Windsor Castle in 2022 is one of the few moments of public unity for William and Harry in recent times. (Mark Kerrison/In Pictures via Getty Images)

custom-made hearse, alongside their father, two uncles, Andrew and Edward, Princess Anne and her husband Tim Laurence, cousin Peter Phillips and David Armstrong-Jones, son of Princess Margaret.

Prince Harry's tribute, with deep affection clear to read, said: "My grandfather was a man of service, honour and great humour. He was authentically himself, with a seriously sharp wit, and could hold the attention of any room due to his charm – and also because you never knew what he might say next."

The next time the princes came together was in July 2021 when they unveiled a statue they had commissioned in the newly created Sunken Garden at Kensington Palace on the anniversary of what would have been Princess Diana's 60th birthday. Covid had once again curtailed the guest list but Diana's two sisters and her brother joined the princes for the ceremony. The statue was designed by British sculptor Ian Rank-Broadley, who also created the two bronze sculptures that decorate the centre of the Armed Forces Memorial at the National Memorial Arboretum in Staffordshire.

It shows Diana accompanied by three children, representing the charities closest to her heart. On a paving stone in front of the statue there are verses adapted from the poem *The Measure of a Man by* an American author, Wallace Gallaher:

"These are the units to measure the worth
Of this woman as a woman regardless of birth.
Not what was her station? But had she a heart?
How did she play her God-given part?"

Appearing relaxed, chatting and smiling with the sculptor, any disagreements between William and Harry were not in evidence. Neither of them spoke formally at the ceremony but they released a statement afterwards: "Today, on what would have been our mother's 60th birthday, we remember her love, strength and character – qualities that made her a force for good around the world, changing countless lives for the better. Every day, we wish she were still with us, and our hope is that this statue will be seen forever as a symbol of her life and her legacy."

When it came time for The Queen's Platinum Jubilee in June 2022, the whole Sussex family arrived from the United States. It was the first time they had introduced their baby daughter Lilibet to her grandparents and great grandparents.

The next uniting event was again a sad one, the funeral of The Queen. Both had official roles to play but they were also mourning the death of their grandmother. It was an emotionally charged day because following The Queen's coffin was reminiscent of the walk the two boys had to make at their mother's funeral. Harry referenced that in a conversation with ITV television interviewer Tom Bradby, when he said: "Just recently my brother and I were walking the same route, and we sort of joked to each other and said: 'At least we know the way'. But otherwise, it was very similar. The only difference was the levels of emotion. Because our grandmother had finished life. There was more, I think, of a celebration and respect and recognition to what she had accomplished. Whereas our mother was taken away far too young." In saying that, Harry identified the one thing that will always unite the princes in a way that no one else can fully appreciate – the love and loss of their mother.

The death of The Queen was quickly followed by Prince Charles' official ascension to the throne as King Charles III. In his first public speech as king, Charles gave William and Catherine the titles of Duke and Duchess of Cornwall and Prince and Princess of Wales and he acknowledged Harry as fifth in line to the throne with his children, Archie and Lilibet, sixth and seventh. "I also wish to express my love for Harry and Meghan as they continue to build their lives overseas," he said. ●

Queen Elizabeth in her prime on a visit to Ottawa, Canada in 2010, leading by example as she did all her life. (Intoit/dreamstime.com)

THE DEATH OF
A QUEEN

One sad event overshadowed all the arguments and bad feeling within the Windsor family. For a while, it took the spotlight off the two princes as it brought the royals, and the country, closer together.

The Queen was the hub of the royal wheel. Around her the whole royal mechanism turned and had done so for 70 years. She set the tone and decided the priorities. She demanded a lot of herself and expected others to follow. Through a life of devotion to the country she had hardly ever raised an eyebrow in anyone or evoked a criticism. Only over the handling of the death of Princess Diana did she attract a negative reaction. But that was not a reaction shared by her grandsons.

For the princes she was a mentor; someone to go to when there was no one else. Often in his memoir Harry talks about telephoning The Queen to discuss a problem or ask for her blessing on something he wants to do. She had been a strong female presence in both boy's lives after the tragic accident that took their mother from them. She had tried to shield them from the fevered press coverage and outpourings of national grief at Diana's death by keeping them with her at Balmoral, but this action had backfired when she was accused of being unfeeling and disrespectful to the Princess by not immediately curtailing the annual holiday.

This was not how the 15-year-old Prince William viewed her. In an interview in 2016 he said: "It's been particularly important to me that I've had somebody like The Queen to look up to and who's been there and who has understood some of the more complex issues when you lose a loved one."

Although it was widely expected to happen in the relatively near future – given The Queen's age of 96 and recent history of failing health – her death still came as a shock to her family, as it would have to any family, and to the British people. For seven decades she had always been there, holding the office of the monarchy in dignified, dutiful hands, riding out the storms and always putting country first, often at the expense of her personal life.

The previous day William and Catherine had taken their children on a preview of what would be their new preparatory school, Lambrook, near Ascot in Berkshire. The term started the following day so when the news came that doctors were warning that The Queen was gravely ill, William made the trip to Balmoral alone. Unfortunately, it took time to arrange a flight with his two uncles and Edward's wife Sophie, and by the time they landed, The Queen had passed away. Fortunately, Prince Charles and his sister Anne were already in Scotland, just a helicopter journey away, so they were able to be by their mother's side at the end.

Harry also failed to make it to Scotland in time, delayed, it was alleged, because he was arguing with his father about his wife accompanying him. In the end he had to charter a flight from Luton, an hour's drive from Windsor, because the commercial flights had ended for the day. He got there that evening and later related how he was able to see her body and speak to her: "I whispered to her that I hoped she was happy, that I hoped she was with Grandpa. I said I was in awe of her carrying out her duties to the last. The Jubilee, the welcoming of a new prime minister."

The Queen probably had the most profound influence on her grandson William as she gently coached him in what he would have to do and how he would be expected to behave as the

The King's Troop Royal Horse Artillery gun carriage flanked by members of the Grenadier Guards takes The Queen on her journey to her lying-in-state in Westminster Hall. (Fred Duval/Shutterstock)

eventual heir to the throne. He acknowledged that in what he said in his public statement immediately after her death: "She was by my side at my happiest moments. And she was by my side during the saddest days of my life. I knew this day would come, but it will be some time before the reality of life without Grannie will truly feel real."

He mentioned the fact that he had benefited from her "wisdom and reassurance", as had Catherine. "My wife has had 20 years of her guidance and support. My three children have got to spend holidays with her and create memories that will last their whole lives.

"I thank her for the kindness she showed my family and me. And I thank her on behalf of my generation for providing an example of service and dignity in public life that was from a different age, but always relevant to us all."

A Dignified Occasion

Despite the disagreements, The Queen's death would draw together all the senior members of the royal family. The death of a monarch is always marked by a lying-in-state followed by a full state funeral. This was something that had been practised covertly for some years before the time came for it to be put into action. All of the close family members had a part in the ceremony, first walking behind the State Gun Carriage carrying The Queen's coffin from Buckingham Palace

to the Palace of Westminster's Hall and then taking a turn at holding a vigil around the coffin as it stood in the Hall. Three days later they accompanied her body to Westminster Abbey for the service and afterwards up the Mall to Hyde Park where a hearse was waiting through the Wellington Arch to take her to her final resting place in St George's Chapel in Windsor.

Much was written about how William and Harry didn't appear to interact during the funeral proceedings and kept eyes focussed ahead as they walked side by side, but as it was a very solemn occasion this was perhaps not surprising. Senior members of the royal family have never displayed strong outward emotion.

However, the two brothers and their wives put on a show of solidarity when they went for a walkabout to see the floral tributes outside the gates of Windsor Castle the evening before the funeral. No one can know if that solidarity was real or staged but perhaps in ways it doesn't matter – it was the royal family doing what The Queen always did: the right thing. ●

William and Catherine, Harry and Meghan stand behind the coffin of The Queen on its arrival at Westminster Hall for the lying-in-state on September 14, 2022. (Darron Fletcher/WPA Pool/Getty Images)

Princess Anne's husband and a former equerry to The Queen, Vice Admiral Sir Timothy Laurence, supports the two princes at their grandmother's funeral. (Patrick van Katwijk/Getty Images)

Sombre looks from Princes William and Harry as The Queen's coffin, draped in the Royal Standard, is carried past by a bearer party from the 1st Battalion Grenadier Guards. (Samir Hussein/WireImage)

A Paddington Bear soft toy with a label saying 'Thank you Ma'am for everything' decorates the railings at Buckingham Palace in memory of The Queen's Platinum Jubilee tea party film which featured the little bear from Peru. (Inkdropcreative1/dreamstime.com)

Prince William and Prince Harry held a vigil at each end of The Queen's catafalque in Westminster Hall, accompanied by six of their cousins. (Aaron Chown/AFP/Getty Images)

THE FUTURE FOR THE
PRINCES

Now separated by the width of an ocean and the entire continent of North America, William and Harry have half a lifetime ahead with, or without, each other.

On May 6, 2023, King Charles and Queen Camilla were crowned. The two royal princes were there to witness their father officially assuming the role of monarch. No doubt what passed through Prince William's mind at some point in the proceedings was that he would one day be taking on that mantle – whether in its present form or in some as yet unknown alternative version. Possible he also wondered if his brother would be beside him at that time.

The history of the monarchy has been peppered with scandals and controversies, defiance of conventions and brotherly rivalries. Overall, though, a sense of duty and service to the British people has prevailed, even at the cost of personal freedoms.

The difference in our modern times has been the ready availability of information, sophisticated PR machines, a plethora of celebrity photographers – authorised and covert – and digital images easily and quickly distributed around the world. The public has lost much of its awe of majesty and developed an appetite for proving that celebrities are just as prone to character flaws and errors of judgment as the rest of us. Providing proof of those human foibles has become a lucrative business and being in possession of a 'scoop', especially one that dishes dirt, has become the holy grail in place of the deferential exclusives that were sought by the press in the past.

In dealing with the modern press the two princes have taken different paths. William is appearing to work very much as his father always has, by negotiation and providing crowd-pleasing good news stories to feed the public appetite and counter any scandal, and by ignoring the rest.

Miguel Head, former Chief Press Officer of the Ministry of Defence, became Private Secretary to Prince William on the resignation of Jamie Lowther-Pinkerton in 2013. Having worked for him for almost 10 years, Head summed up Prince William's approach. "He is an incredibly moral guy... He knows he's playing a long game; he's in this job for the rest of his life and doesn't need to get short-term bonus points. He's got enough confidence in his own integrity and character that by doing the right thing he will earn the respect he wants. He takes after his grandmother in that respect... She's never done anything to court public opinion, nothing populist, always played things incredibly straight, and he sees her life and marriage as a model."

In contrast, Prince Harry has set an objective to fight the injustices of the press towards himself and his wife by mounting legal challenges. His overall aim seems to be to force a change in the approach to celebrity that will benefit everyone who currently suffers from being spied on covertly and written about in unfairly derogatory terms. *Guardian* newspaper columnist Zoe Williams summed it up in an article just before the coronation. "... it's always been quite fundamental to the tabloids' power

that, in the absence of a fresh scandal, they can generate a propulsive narrative by pitting one member of the family against another – Diana against Camilla, Kate against Meghan, William against Harry, bold splashes of black and white in which the reader is invited to pick their team... I think, in the long run, it [Harry's pursuit of three British newspaper groups through the UK courts in 2023] will be worth it: in two years' time we won't be able to remember what we were supposed to dislike about the couple."

As for the rift between the brothers, in 2019 Prince Harry responded in an ITV interview to reports of a breakdown of relations with his brother William: "We are brothers. We will always be brothers. We are certainly on different paths at the moment but I will always be there for him as I know he will always be there for me."

At their father's coronation the two princes were very much apart in Westminster Abbey, separated by half a dozen people and a row of seats, and by their different arrival and departure times. The solemnity of the occasion and their location also precluded any personal conversation or even an exchange of glances. Whether they met up the day before, when Harry flew in from the States, is not something that has been revealed and he left for the airport and the return flight directly after the ceremony, so opportunities would have been limited.

So, the coronation may have re-set the clock for the princes, or it may have signalled a final parting. Only time will tell. ●

Prince William and Prince Harry share a warm glance at the opening of a sports centre for disadvantaged children in 2018. (Toby Melville/WPA Pool/Getty Images)